[REAL]

[REAL]

The 30-Day
Social Media Movement

Leah Young

WESTBOW
PRESS®
A DIVISION OF THOMAS NELSON
& ZONDERVAN

WestBow Press books may be ordered through booksellers or by contacting:

WestBow Press
A Division of Thomas Nelson & Zondervan
1663 Liberty Drive
Bloomington, IN 47403
www.westbowpress.com
1 (866) 928-1240

ISBN: 978-1-5127-3817-9 (sc)
ISBN: 978-1-5127-3818-6 (hc)
ISBN: 978-1-5127-3816-2 (e)

Library of Congress Control Number: 2016906169

Print information available on the last page.

WestBow Press rev. date: 5/5/2016

Thank You

Lord - this book and this movement would not exist
without You. Thank You for giving us an identity.

To those who took this challenge with me in the very beginning,
and to all those who are taking it or have yet to take it – you
are the REAL deal. It's an honor to tell your stories.

To Andrew – you've been there from the start, and you're still here.
Thank you for never giving up on me and for believing in my story.
I love you.

Contents

Introduction:
Where It All Started

You can't tell anyone what I'm about to tell you.

"Ok, I promise, I won't."

Like, seriously ... NO ONE!

"I would never. Just tell me, what's going on?"

I can't even believe I'm about to tell you this.

"Why not? You know you can trust me."

I know that but it's still scary. Not that you'll tell anyone, but what you'll think of me after I tell you. That's why I don't want anyone to know. I don't want them to see me differently.

* * *

This was a real conversation with a real person.

I won't document her name or the rest of the conversation, but those last few words she said to me will always be with me: *I don't want them to see me differently.* I've been in the same place my friend was in that moment, feeling isolated and terrified of rejection. Maybe you've been there too?

The near-to-worst part about that conversation was that I thought I knew who this person was; I thought I had her pinned down. The worst

1

part about it was that I thought she knew who I was too. I was painfully mistaken.

Here's what I can tell you about this girl I thought I knew. She was the life of the party, the carefree, in your face, "I don't-care-what-anyone-thinks-about-me" kind of girl. The girl who could make you laugh till you cried. The girl who came into church every Sunday, sang at the top of her lungs during the song set, raised her hands to pray out loud, and smiled at people as she walked through the lobby. Despite a rough past, she was making strides towards a bright future.

Several months later, we stood beneath flickering lights outside of a coffee shop. She held back tears of regret, admitting mistakes she thought no one else would dare ever make to an individual she thought was completely perfect.

Here's who she thought I was, and who you might have thought I was too if we had chanced to meet:

My name is Leah.

I've grown up going to church because it's what my family has always done, from my parents to all nine of my siblings. Yes, nine siblings. We're all one, giant, happy family. Every single one of us is unique and gifted, which only adds to my social ranking. I mean, if you come from a good, Christian family tree, you must be a bright, red apple, ripe for selection, right?

From the time I could form recognizable syllables, I was singing ... or, at the time, melodically yelling. But as the years progressed, so did my ability to harmonize and project notes. That ability soon landed me the job of my dreams. Immediately out of a drama-free, homeschooled high-school

2

education, I found myself accepting a position as the Worship Director for my local church. If that doesn't earn a good, Christian girl a few gold stars, I don't know what does!

As I did my best to juggle song sets and rehearsals, I also managed to pursue a degree in English to further add to my list of growing accomplishments. Even with my over-committed scheduled, I somehow didn't let my social life suffer.

I dated around all in the "pursuit" of Prince Charming's second cousin. At least then I could find the "perfect mate" and wouldn't be crucified for "setting my standards too high." At one time, I even sported a sparkly purity ring just to rub in the faces of all the singles out there.

My other "social hobbies" included, but were not limited to, a quaint little word I liked to misuse: *mentorship*. Just about every week, I met a new young woman at a coffee shop or took them out to breakfast where they could cry over past mistakes and I could respond with, *"How do you feel about that?"* Very therapeutic, I'm sure.

Aside from my Sunday morning responsibilities, I grow eight other arms (metaphorically speaking, of course), and started helping out in various places around the church to put myself out there in the religious spotlight. Youth ministry, young adult ministry, administration, missions trips, videography, set design – you name it, my name was either on the sign-up sheet or underneath the title of *Leader*.

Not only was I on the stage, underneath bright lights and illuminated choruses of our congregation's favorite songs, I was underneath the spotlight of everyone's attention. I waved my Christian girl magic wand over the social media platforms I frequented, mainly Facebook (www.

facebook.com) and Instagram (www.instagram.com). I didn't get on the Twitter (www.twitter.com) bandwagon until later. It was over all of these that you could either read passionate statuses or look at filtered pictures of "who I was."

Me. Me. Me.

Here's a picture with my loving family. Here's a picture with friends as we head out to a three-day, Christian conference. Here's a picture of my new Beth Moore Bible study, while I casually sip on my white chocolate mocha. Here's a picture of the orphans I sponsor in Africa. Here's a picture of my pristine outfits, complete with a blemish-free complexion, even first thing in the morning. Here I am working out because my body is a temple. Here I am traveling to another country because I must "go into all the world." Here I am saving the world because …

My name is Leah, and *I'm perfect*.

That's the person you would see if you knew me because that's whom I would let you see.

After considering all of this being shoved in people's faces, it shouldn't seem odd that I would get a text from this life-of-the-party girl, asking to meet with me at a coffee shop. That's just what I did. In fact, she and I had been meeting regularly for several months and it was always the same. We met. She talked. I listened and nodded. I quoted some Scripture or gave blunt advice. She nodded and sipped her coffee. We'd smile and leave. But this time was different.

Our conversation took us from our comfy seats inside to the parking lot outside. As the employees locked the doors and drove home, we stood next to our cars, with red faces and tears in our eyes. We met. She talked.

I listened. She confessed some things. I stopped smiling. I listened more. We cried. We hugged. We left. That time was different.

I can't document the conclusion of that conversation because that story is hers to share. What I can tell you is that what she shared with me that night changed my life. One conversation changed my life because it changed my perspective. I thought I knew who she was. I thought I knew who I was.

As I drove home that night, digging my nails into my steering wheel, angrily swiping away tears, I yelled at God. I yelled at God for most of the drive home. I had never done that before because the idea just seemed blasphemous. But this time was different.

"How could this happen to her? Why did this happen to her? How could all of this escape my notice? We've been meeting together for months!" I yelled and cried. "Why didn't she say anything? How did I miss it? Why did You let me miss it? Why didn't You stop it?"

Finally I shut up long enough to hear God speak to me. I can count on one hand the number of times I've heard the Lord speak to me. That night was one of those times.

You've missed all of this because you've been missing her. You missed her because you don't know how to see people, really see them. How was she supposed to tell you anything real? How would you have seen it? How can you truly see and know the people around you when you're so consumed with gaining approval for yourself?

I bit my lip. "God, what can I do to fix this?"

This is everywhere. People miss other people because they're too busy with themselves. They're too busy trying to create an identity that isn't theirs. Just look at the world of social media! It's everywhere. No one knows who they truly are. No one knows their real identities.

As I thought about it, I realized that I was doing it, and nearly everyone I followed on social media was doing it too.

"It's like we think we have to be perfect all the time," I continued. "It's like who we really are isn't good enough."

Is perfection approachable? Is it REAL?

My car reached the driveway, and those words reached my heart.

Have you ever just been *done?* I was done. I wasn't quite sure what that looked like or what it would take, but I knew in that moment that I was done. I was done pretending. I was done lugging around a bag of masks. I was done believing the lies and portraying them to my followers on social media. I was done being fake. I was done faking *who I really am.*

Before I wrote all of this, before anything called "The [REAL] 30-Day Challenge" surfaced, a painful, yet crucial awakening needed to take place in the heart of a young woman who didn't really know herself. That's me. This is my story of identity.

My name is Leah, and I'm not perfect. I'm ready to be REAL.

What is [REAL]?

Who are you?

Very few people can honestly answer that question. Some people will spend their whole lives trying to answer that question. Some people will die for the sake of answering that question.

Everyone on earth is seeking the answer. This is the crux of the matter – of all human matter.

Why is it so hard to find the answer?

I believe it's because **things have lost their original meaning**. Let me explain.

In my opinion, English is the most inconsistent language. I had to spend hours sitting in a classroom learning about it and writing papers on it. Isn't it odd that we have a degree based on our own language? Think of the words we use.

We are horrified by murder, yet we jokingly say we want to "kill" the person who annoys or messes with us. On one end we'll apply a negative connotation to words like *stinking*, *destroyed*, *bad*, or *insane*, but on another end, we'll use the same words to describe events or people who amaze or impress us: *that vocalist absolutely destroyed that song!* We *love* our spouses, our children, our family members, and our friends, but we also *love* coffee, zombie movies, and sleeping in.

Please don't think I'm suggesting that we completely revamp the English language. This is just to prove a point: words have lost their original meanings.

The same goes for **people**.

People are no longer defined by *who they are* but rather what they do, what they own, what college they attended, what degree they received, where they've been, who they know, how much money they make … and the list goes on.

Think about this.

You're in a conversation with a friend and happen to mention your friend *Zach* (let's just go with that). But the person you're talking to doesn't know Zach, and so naturally, that person asks, *"Who is Zach?"*

There's the question.

Consider how you might answer that question. Like most people, you'd probably start with Zach's physical appearance: brown hair, brown eyes, dark skin. You might continue with Zach's background and influence: attends this school, majors in this degree, comes from this family, is friends with this person, is dating this person, works at this place. If you're really good friends with Zach or have an attraction to him, you might expound even further on what you know about his personality or personal achievements: has a kind heart, is sociable, heads up this social activist club on campus, started this movement, wrote this book, etc.

So, *that's* Zach. Right?

It might serve as a fitting *description* for Zach so that other people can identify him, but that's not what defines *who* he is.

If this is how we continue to define who people are, and who we are, it becomes a frightening reality.

It's frightening because we're *human*. Unlike the portrait of perfection that the media paints and society tells us we need to achieve, **human beings are incredibly flawed.** We will never obtain that perfection this side of eternity, and we will only commit slow suicide trying.

What if I described *Claire** to you in this way? Well, she recently battled a fierce type of cancer that zapped away at her life.

What about *Martin?* * He's a recovering alcoholic and is trying to regain custody of his children.

What about *Addy?* * She's addicted to pornography and has completely separated herself from her family because of the shame.

All of the above names are fictitious to protect the identities of real people.

Are these people any less worthy than *Zach* just because they're sick, struggling, or trapped? Are people any less worthy when circumstances, their appearance, or their background doesn't fit the social "perfection" quota?

What is it that we, as a society, are missing?

That question sparked something inside of me that birthed a dream. The byproduct of that dream is now a social media movement known as **"The [REAL] 30-Day Challenge."**

We probably don't know each other, and we may never meet, but the book you hold is something very personal. It is the documentation of a powerful and life-changing journey that I and many other people decided to take. It started as a means of self-discovery and the tool God used to change my heart. It turned into an invitation for others to do it for themselves. It has now become the start of a movement, one, that I pray, will go global. But to even become what it is today, it had to take on one of the most widely used platforms in today's world: **social media.**

I love social media. For the most part, I have nothing against it. I hope you'll remember that as you continue reading.

Most of us have our preference, but I think many more people are catching onto Instagram because visuals are powerful and interactive, and there are few limits to what people can do with an image they capture. People are even uploading their professional photography to Instagram! Why is that?

The answer is simple: **it gathers attention.**

Double-tap the screen or press the "like" button and you've just made someone's day. I don't think I'm exaggerating. Think about the reason you upload your photos to Instagram. I know why I do it: I want the people who are connected with me, and the people I can reach through hashtags, to affirm the places I go, the things I like to do, the clothes I wear, the way I look, the people I'm around, etc.

It's all about affirmation and approval.

Obviously I'm not trying to prove an issue with Instagram because I use it too. I think all social media sites have the potential for great things. There are so many people utilizing social media to encourage and inspire others, target real issues, and raise a voice for those who have none. **But social**

media also has the potential to be used for selfish intent. I found myself leaning toward that side.

Rewind to the introduction of this book. That was where my ah-ha moment happened. It was a cruel, painful ah-ha moment, but I'm so thankful it happened. That moment was when God asked me one of the hardest questions I've ever been asked: *How can you truly see and know the people around you when you're so consumed with gaining approval for yourself?*

One of the biggest problems with social media is that we can control exactly what others will learn about us and they can control exactly what we will learn about them. We can create our own reality and vice versa. **We can mask the real truth and at the same time deceive ourselves into thinking the people we're viewing on social media are perfect.**

We think we need to dress ourselves up with filters and rehearsed smiles so that our followers stay entertained and keep handing us these imaginary digital hearts that say, "I like it!" Meanwhile, our own hearts are struggling to breathe, drowning beneath another wave of fabrication.

Social media does exactly what the name implies - it provides a *means* to be social. It has the power to connect virtually anyone, anywhere, at any time; however, it lacks the personal power of real relationships. As a society, we've come to accept social media as a new level of communication and connection, turning it into a substitute for real relationships.

Our lives have become so closely connected, and yet the "intimacy" we feel we're receiving is counterfeit.

Is that too harsh? I'm just trying to keep it real. If we're honest, we admit that, as fantastic a platform as social media is, *we're missing something*.

Facebook is nice, but it doesn't beat real **face-to-face time.**

Twitter is nice, but 140 characters should never suffice for **wholesome conversation.**

Instagram is nice, but **life isn't filtered, isn't perfect, isn't glamorous all the time.**

Sadly, with social media sites like Instagram, we get stuck in playing this comparison game. Why is that? I think it's because all that's pictured for us to view is what's glamorous or attractive; **no one is going to post the stuff that *really* happened.** And because visuals are such a powerful thing, we end up creating this fantasy world in our heads. It consists of two different worlds: the world we see others living in and the ideal world we create for ourselves.

Remember my moment with the girl I thought I knew? Her deepest fear wasn't that I would tell someone about the mistakes she had made but of what people would think after the fact … of what *I, her friend,* would think after the fact.

All of the real stuff gets left out because we're afraid.

We're afraid that if people see us for who we really are, or see what we like to do, or see our mistakes, or whatever it might be, they'll disapprove … they'll walk away. **Rejection is something we dread.** We forget that the people we're following on Instagram, Facebook, or any other social media site are real people who are messy, sloppy, weak, and imperfect, just like us. They face real struggles. They desire things we do. They experience pain. It's not a bad thing to want to show off the blessed stuff in your life or take an occasional "selfie." **It's when it starts to drown out the real stuff that it becomes an issue**.

Not everything should get posted for the entire world to see. But I wonder if we were real with each other over social media, even for just a *day,* how different would our lives look to others tuning in? What kind of effect would it have on other people? Would they really walk away, shaking their heads and casting a judgmental glance in our direction? We fear they would. But I argue that more often than what we think, people would be inspired … encouraged … challenged … moved … empowered … set free … healed … maybe even transformed.

Is it possible that our authenticity – a quality that is rare in technology – could give people hope? Could it build their self-confidence? Could it save a life, hanging in the balance of rejection and past pain?

I'm not saying that social media is evil. With the Lord's help, I've recognized that I've idolized social media. I used social media for selfish intent and that's where social media goes downhill.

What changed for me? Rewind to that evening with my friend.

As soon as I got home, I grabbed a blank sheet of paper and a pen. Nothing came to me right away. I could barely sleep that night because all I could think about was what would go on that piece of paper. I didn't find out until the next day. At a few minutes past nine in the morning, I sat down at my kitchen table and wrote out *exactly* what I heard the Lord tell me to write.

Here's the outcome:

Since photo challenges are a "thing" on Instagram, God gave me one called, "The [REAL] 30-Day Challenge." This challenge was going to rock my world. It was going to open up my heart and dig up all the stuff I had buried for years.

The rules were simple: no filters, no manipulation, black and white photos only. Each day had a different theme designed to dig deep and expose parts of an individual that might otherwise go untouched.

I was terrified but excited all at the same time. I wanted to change. I wanted to be real. Even though I had no idea what to expect, I was ready. But then something incredible and unscripted happened. After just one day of surfacing over my personal Instagram account, guys and girls started to respond, asking to join in the challenge with me. Of course I was happy to have them join me. After only a week, I started to see my feed fill up with stunning black and white pictures, **as people began to respond to the call to be truly real with each other.**

Regardless of their intent with taking the challenge, I started to see complete strangers post that first picture of myself holding up the sign. I started using the hashtag **#REAL30daychallenge** and so other people started doing it too. Because of the hashtag page, we could easily see what was being shared! The hashtag page went from 100 pictures to 1,000 pictures in just 30 days.

Without any prompting from me, people started connecting through the hashtag page. They were reading each other's stories; rejoicing over each other's successes; mourning with each other over failures, losses, and struggles; and, offering encouragement and grace over difficult addictions and past mistakes. **It was heartwarming to see complete strangers connecting with each other over similar issues and realizing they were not alone.** To see people, once filling up their feeds with "selfies" or cute animals or what they had for dinner now posting pictures of their struggles, their victories, their dreams, people they admired, and so much more. To see people posting pictures of real issues and speaking out against things like abortion, child abuse, the sex trade industry, homelessness, and poverty.

I was left speechless.

Therefore, since my mouth had nothing more to say, my fingers decided to start talking. I started up a blog to document my own journey and highlight the journeys of those who had dared to take the challenge with me. Every ten days, I would compile these pictures and stories onto the blog so that people could see just what was taking place over Instagram. The response was incredible.

Every few days, I would receive emails and messages on Facebook from people who were taking the challenge. The content varied from a simple *thank you* to a detailed testimony of what was happening in their lives because of "The [REAL] 30-Day Challenge." I couldn't stop smiling whenever I received a success story about how it was impacting a life in a positive way. Sometimes the emails brought me to tears as I was allowed to know about hidden secrets that had gone unspoken for years, until now.

"Because you've dared to be real, it has inspired me to be real too." This was the common response that kept me going, reminding me that it was worth it even for just one person.

Rediscovering authenticity was awakening us to our identities. With that knowledge and empowerment, our lives were being transformed and it was all evidenced by the stunning black and whites that were slowly emerging. But don't just take my word for it.

See for yourself just what took place with "The [REAL] 30-Day Challenge."

The Breakdown

Before I dive into the challenge, here's a breakdown of some of the features of Instagram for those that are unfamiliar.

Because this challenge is all about being real, I want to document my journey exactly as it happened and authentically display what you would have seen if you had been following it on Instagram. I can't duplicate everything as is, so please excuse me if you're an "Instagram veteran." Everything you're going to read has been taken directly from my personal Instagram and the accounts of others who joined in on the challenge.

Every portion of this book is separated by the days of the challenge. Each one is labeled just as it is on the sign I created for the challenge (ex: Day 20 - What Inspires Me).

After that you have the image. Each image had to be posted using the following stipulations: black and white only, no filters, and no manipulations. I didn't edit the pictures before I posted them and took all of them using my iPhone. Instagram offers a wide range of filters to enhance your photos. I understand that there is a black and white filter but this does nothing to enhance the photo, just void it of color. I didn't manipulate the photos - no cleaning things up or moving them around to look good.

Next you have my username. I'd like to note that I've included the username I had when this challenge first surfaced. I got married since that's happened so, therefore, my username has changed.

Beneath every photo, there is the option to enter a caption. The caption is an important element of the challenge. Every photo tells a story, but the caption tells what the picture cannot. The captions should never be so long that they detract from the photo.

Underneath the caption, you have what I referred to earlier as "digital hearts." The heart represents the number of "likes" you can receive from other Instagram users. If they like what you post, they can hit the "like" button or double-tap their smartphone screen. The number of "likes" usually indicates how much attention your photo is receiving, but it's not entirely indicative of the amount of views.

Finally, you have the comments box. It allows other users to go even further than liking your photo. They can let you know what they're thinking, feeling, etc. Their username pops up next to their comment. To secure the identity of any users on my personal Instagram account (those who wish to remain anonymous), I have excluded their usernames. Instead I've used ☺ to separate the comments that were posted to each of my pictures.

The picture posts that follow each of mine in *The Response* sections have been submitted with permission for me to use, and for that I'm so thankful; to be able to tell these stories is an honor.

Hashtags (#) are an easy way for users on Instagram, Twitter, and Facebook to locate similar items or market similar items. Once something is hash-tagged, it creates a folder for it. The more one phrase or word is hash-tagged, the more the folder will fill up with those associated images. It has the potential to become its own community. It has the ability to link people together even more than before and that's exactly what happened for "The [REAL] 30-Day Challenge."

Now that you have the Breakdown, let's dive right in.

This is my story. This is their story. This is our story.

Day 1:
Fresh Face Selfie

leahmarieball:

What girl would ever want to upload a photo of herself when she's tired, no make-up, just "bumming it", and maybe dealing with a breakout or two? This was a tough one for me because that description fits me in this picture. I love make-up and don't think there's anything wrong with it provided that you're confident enough in the face God gave you. I think make-up should only be viewed as a way to bring attention to features of you that are already beautiful! I'm thankful for my eyes, so I like to use make-up to enhance what God has already given me. I'm more self-conscious of my nose because it's sensitive and turns red in the Florida heat. But I'm learning to love these things about myself that 1) I can't change, 2) are apart of what makes me unique, and 3) because it's how God intended for me to look. I stayed away from make-up on this day. Sometimes we need to break away from certain routine things to be able to evaluate if they have more control over us than we do of them.

41 people like this

<u>**Comments**</u>:

☺ You have always been so beautiful my friend ... Inside and out ;-)

☺   Wow! You're so beautiful my friend! Love this and so excited on what you're doing and how you've encouraged me and others to do the same. ♥

☺   Gah. A challenge. I accept. #braceyoself

☺   Wow, I don't think I would have enough guts to post a picture of myself without makeup.

☺   I'm doing this!

☺   It might be a bit late, but you're such an inspiration. I was scrolling through your profile. And it's good to see people like you ... who are still so grounded and down to earth. It's nice to see someone who still has good moral values and isn't self-absorbed in small problems. People like you who generally stress the issues of the society even if it's just on an Instagram page. It's good to see someone who has been through a really rough time and made it out stronger than ever. I'm going to take the #real30daychallenge.

Day 1:
Fresh Face Selfie

The Response

These are only a few of the brave guys and girls that dared to post a picture of their faces without make-up, touch-ups, filters, or manipulation. I wish I could have collected every face, but since this book has been completed, more and more have been added. These are faces of confidence, strength, and authenticity.

These are the types of people who cause you to feel comfortable whenever you're around them because they're comfortable in their own skin. Without any masks or reasons to hide, these are the types of people that connect with others because right from the start, we feel safe, we feel invited into their circle, and we feel worth it in our own skin.

Day 2:
An Unspoken
Dream

leahmarieball:

I often imagine myself doing many things, but one that comes up a lot is speaking in front of large crowds at churches or conferences. Mainly I see myself speaking to women or young adults and youth. Not as a pastor but as an author. So this dream is two-fold - to write books or curriculum for those audiences and then speak on them. It's not to be a speaker, more like a communicator.

24 people like this

Comments:

☺   My unspoken dream is one day helping troubled teenagers with their problems!!! All they want is for someone to find them important and show them that they are not alone in their troubles!!! I want to be that person ... I haven't always had that so I want to do that for someone ... I want to make a difference in someone's life!!! :)

Day 2:
An Unspoken Dream

The Response

Everyone has a dream. Some of them are communicated openly, some of them are concealed because we've been told they're too big … too extravagant … too expensive … too impossible. So if all of that were true about your dream, what's the point in letting it go public?

The point is to remind yourself why you dreamt it in the first place. The point is to inspire other people to start dreaming for themselves. And finally, speaking it out loud gives it life. What we do with it next is entirely up to us.

beccadempsey: In 2008 I went on my first mission's trip, which forever changed my life. While on that trip I had the opportunity to go to an orphanage. There for the first time my eyes were opened to a way of life that I had never known. For a child so small to be left alone, with no family, no place to call home, and leaving them with no hope. But as I hugged them and let them sit on my lap, I watched hope flood their eyes. Given the opportunity, one day I would love to work with orphans in Africa, bringing them the hope and love of Christ.

anonymous: Eleven years ago I watched helplessly as my sister turned her life, our family, and her relationships upside-down as a result of drug use and addiction. Since then I've experienced people close to me whom I love with my whole heart be overtaken by this merciless addiction. My heart has been angry, broken, and bitter for the people I love and the ones I barely know. My unspoken dream is to one day create a safe haven for teens to young adult-aged addicts who are struggling with substance abuse. I want to create a place where recovering addicts dare to dream again ... a place where their future is full of hope and restoration rather than pain and brokenness. Part of my dream is partnering with my sister who I believe will have the most amazing testimony when she takes the final steps out of her chains.

heyyyyash: My unspoken dream … to mentor young girls, specifically in regards to self-esteem and having a healthy self-image. For it to be my full-time job and have my 40-hour work week mean more than just the dollar amount on my paycheck. For my sphere of influence and ripple into eternity to be more significant than what is typically measured as the standard of "success" (I.e. salary, career advancement, etc.).

_jassminenicole: My unspoken dream would be to lead worship and minister to the deaf community.

Day 3:
Someone I
Secretly Admire

leahmarieball:

I haven't known her long, but she's one of those people that, after you talk
with her over coffee, you feel like you've known her for years. There's so
much about [this person] that I admire: her honesty, her love for the Lord, her
leadership, her abandonment in worship, her voice / talent, her quiet / gentle
beauty, how authentic she is, her humor, her wisdom, even her style (oh hey,
hipster chick). I'm blessed to call her my friend and sister in Christ. She has
taught me a lot in just a few years about what it means to be a worshipper of
the King in every aspect of our lives. Love yah girl ;)

35 people like this

Comments:

☺ Amen to all of this.

☺   She sounds like a gem!

☺   Wow ... way to make me tear up Leah! What an encouragement coming from you. I really needed this today friend. Love you and we need to have some coffee together soon.

Day 3:
Someone I
Secretly Admire

The Response

People we secretly admire are usually the ones who actually need to hear the most that we love and appreciate them. These people are pouring out so much that they need to be filled every once in a while. They need to be told that they're making a difference in the lives of others, even if their contribution is seemingly behind the scenes.

I think we get so hung up on our own pride and the fear of what others might think that we keep quiet about these people and what they really mean to us. Day 3 taught all of us not to hold back. Our reward was making someone else's day.

Jazzy_pedraza: Elissa Lee. Known by many, loved by all. This woman is always giving her all for Christ. You can hear her passion with every note ringing from her mouth. Every word that exits...She's always there to tell me, 'Shut up and sing.' (okay...maybe it's a bit sweeter. SOMETIMES.) When I feel I can't do it or I am not good at a part. She can give sweet words or stern. It's all dependent on what's needed. She is always willing to drop anything she's doing and help anyone out. She's a great role model and worship leader. She is always there for everyone. Quickly able to bring a smile to your face, pray for you, or give you a quick word of encouragement. This is Elissa, a woman I admire.

lilyanaabril: Someone I secretly admire would be my Titi Juanita. She is incredible. Honestly. She puts her whole heart into everything she does, she has a great voice, and her love for God is amazing. One of my favorite things about her is that she tells it like it is, because honestly that's what people need sometimes. She has helped so many people, given so much great advice. She is very wise and levelheaded. She is just a great person overall, inside and out. I admire all that she does and who she is. I love you Titi.

iix.sydneylee: I really don't think this is a secret, but this is one wonderful woman. My French teacher, Madame C. I've been studying French half my life and she's been there every step of the way. She has known me ever since I was a dorky little kid, barely able to ask how someone was in French. Determined, patient, and kind-hearted are some of the best words to describe her. Madame C. continually teaches me to never give up and to always strive for the best.

Day 4:
What Really
Happened

leahmarieball:

It was a Wednesday last year, and during our church staff meeting, I started doodling when I should have been taking notes. I drew this picture and snapped a photo. I was exhausted that day and drank more coffee than I should have. Everybody thought I was working extra hard, what with all my responsibilities at work and school. But what really happened was more than I was willing to admit. I was depressed, bitter, struggling, and in my indifference, I had gotten wasted the night before and hadn't slept but maybe two hours. That wasn't like me at all. But there it is. During that time, I just stopped caring because I felt like I had failed - so why try anymore? I'm so thankful that when I'm unfaithful, He is abundantly faithful.

40 people like this

Comments:

☺   That was so encouraging, ma. Thank you. #respect

☺   You're an inspiration, lady! Brave, bold, and beautiful soul!

☺   You are a beautiful, transparent, real, and unwavering human being, my dear.

Day 4:
What Really
Happened

The Response

They say "a picture is worth a thousand words" but those pictures can often lie to us. There are so many times we post pictures or say things on social media that don't truly tell the entire story. Whether it's to cover up the truth or fake it for someone else's sake, it's not worth it in the long run to have a gallery of seemingly spotless pictures.

Do we want people to feel defeated when they look through our pictures because they'll never have such a fun, carefree life? Or do we want them to realize we're just normal people too? When we choose to show the real deal instead of fabricated fantasies, what really happens is that people can see us for who we truly are, and in turn, embrace their own humanity.

anonymous: This picture was taken a few years ago when I was finishing up middle school and was just starting off into high school. This point in my life was a pretty horrible time that I try to block out of my memories. I dreaded school. Hated it actually. I didn't understand anything at all, not even my teachers could help me understand a "simple" math problem. I started cheating just to pass with a C-. My home life was more like a war zone it felt like at times. My parents hit a rough patch in their marriage that my mom actually left for months. She didn't visit a whole lot, but when she did come back home, I'd hear her knocking over things in the middle of the night because she was too drunk to even walk in a straight path. My "love" life wasn't what I thought it was. I based my happiness off a boy that made me feel like I actually mattered. But, soon enough, he left me heart broken. I really didn't enjoy life anymore. I couldn't sleep nor could I eat at all, and if I did, it would not stay down. I hated myself so much. I felt worthless, stupid, ugly, unlovable, alone, and so much more. I sat in my room and cried and thought of ways to take away the pain I felt. Cutting became the answer. After a while, it didn't help anymore and thoughts of suicide crept in. My dad noticed I wasn't myself the one day and asked me to tag along while he ran some errands just to get out of the house. I went and sat in the truck more than half the time while he went into the store. Sitting there listening to the radio, a song came on called "You Are More" [by Tenth Avenue North]. Listening to the lyrics made tears fill my eyes. I felt the presence of God there with me. Those words coming out from the song made me feel like God wasn't going to give up on me, nor will He ever. I gave God another chance that night and I finally felt like I was actually living life once again.

cassiedassie: I was walking down the boardwalk with my DR family and we noticed this perfect hipster couple, so I wanted a picture with them. After following them for a few seconds, I turned around so you could only see their backs, but mister hipster noticed and was less than pleased.

anonymous: This was a time in my life where I was going through a lot and became pretty depressed. I lost a lot of weight due to stress and anxiety and I was hurting and therefore started hurting others ... especially [my sister]. [My mom always wanted us to take a cute picture together, smiling and happy], but I'm pretty sure we got into a huge fight about five minutes later. I had gotten angry about something stupid like many depressed people do. I ended up in the bathroom crying because I was in this position where I was hurting people I love even when I didn't want to be. I'm so thankful for God's grace and that He can turn a crappy situation around and bring it to glorify Him. I'm also thankful for a sister who never gave up on me and who has dealt with me through the bad and the good.

Day 5:
Outside My
Front Door

leahmarieball:

Our yard has seen a dramatic transition over the years as we've gone through swing sets for my siblings, tree houses, forts, my dad's carpentry, my mom's flowers, my brother's ... contraptions. But the one thing that has been here since we moved in has been the Bottlebrush tree with its bright red blossoms, and a few years after, my dad put in this swing. It has been the place for many tears, late-night conversations, writing sessions, the perfect reading nook, and prayer spot. It's my favorite place to pray and read my Bible. It's like an invitation right when I step outside my front door.

25 people like this

<u>Comments:</u>

None.

Day 5:
Outside My
Front Door

The Response

Where a person lives is a picture of where that individual came from: his or her past, background, childhood, etc. It's a glimpse into what that person sees every morning in his or her present and how that person will let it shape the next few steps out the door into the future.

Outside our front doors there might be many memories we wish we could forget or those we wish to hold onto for years to come. But every story has a purpose. These are the stories we should tell.

missmaddieroseee: My parents decided to have nine children. Those children have lots of friends. Those friends are little people for the most part. I find it painfully ironic that the choice of plant outside my front door is a cactus. Like it's on the ground … not on a shelf or hidden and out of reach. The temptation we all face to touch this cactus is unbearable.

Seriously though, God put a lot of detail into this plant. Look at every design, the texture, the size, and the uniqueness. God spent time on this little baby plant. You are a million times more beautifully defined, and thought out than this little cactus outside my door. I love nature. It not only shows off God's incredible artistry, but how much more He loves you. Your heart is 20x more detailed than my little baby cactus. I love this cactus … I still find it really funny though.

rachlovesjoy: This may seem like a typical neighborhood, a typical picture, nothing special … but to me this picture represents so much more. This is the view I see when I greet my husband as he comes home after a long day of work. This is where I go to look at the mountains off in the distance when I am seeking peace and quiet. This is where I hope to see my future children's smiling faces as they play in the front yard or take their first steps. This is the view from my front door, the view of my present and my future. This is where my heart is, where my home is.

iamhisart: WE LITERALLY MOVED ACROSS THE STREET. The house directly across from us was the last place we ever rented. My mom was so happy to finally own a house for herself. Yeah, renting came with its problems: not being able to decorate, sometimes not being allowed to have pets, and annoying landlords, but I'm thankful for our humble beginnings. Renting wasn't always glamorous, but it has shown me that love is what makes a home, not the size of it.

Day 6:
Secret Jam

leahmarieball:

I'm a hopeful romantic, what can I say? I love romantic movies, and Disney© movies! The soundtracks aren't half bad. I'm not blasting it in my car on the way to work (it's hard to get pumped to classical ... at least for me), but I really like the song "I See the Light" from Disney's *Tangled*... it makes me think of a romantic relationship, but as odd as this sounds, it reminds me how empty and dull life is without Christ. When Christ came into my life, everything ignited - "all at once everything is different, now that I see you."

28 people like this

Comments:

☺ Judging you. #jk

Day 6:
Secret Jam

The Response

I like Justin Bieber's music. I like the old Backstreet Boys songs. If you happened to play "A Whole New World" from the Disney movie, *Aladdin*, plug … your … ears!

A secret jam isn't the key to a person's deepest, darkest secrets, but it DOES hold the key to a portion of their personality that they might be afraid to reveal. For example, guys that dig Alicia Keys, girls that can't stop blaring Journey - it's indicative of something secretly sensitive that otherwise comes off rough, or something secretly playful that comes off guarded. Time to turn up the music and let those walls come down!

therealcorysullivan: So, I don't really hide anything musically. Everyone knows that I listen to everything from pop, rock, country, hip-hop, R&B, etc. What is probably pretty lame though is that ["I'll Make a Man Out of You" from Disney's *Mulan* Soundtrack] has legit been on my gym playlist since I was about 18. Something about this song just pumps me up and gets me ready for the war against myself. A war against the childish ideas of giving up when it gets hard, not only in the gym, but in every area of life. Sometimes you have to man up and do the things that you and others thought would never be possible. Giving up is never an option.

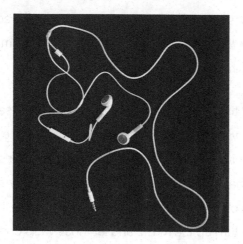

Therealandrewyoung: My secret jam is "Story of My Life" by One Direction. The first time I heard it, I wasn't a fan, but my fiancée insisted on listening to it over and over. It has become my secret jam.

Day 7:
Portrait of a
Real Person

leahmarieball:

This is my friend Shandi. She looks like a cartoon character, which actually fits her personality perfectly. Anyone who first meets her is laughing within five minutes of the conversation. She has the ability to get you thinking about yourself in ways that you never have before. Because she's so genuine, so determined in her pursuit of righteousness, her actions are often questioned - "Is this chick for real?" Yeah, she is :) and I'm proud/blessed to call her one of my friends. She's creative, nurturing, and makes incredible sacrifices for her family every day, especially her sisters. She has seen pain and abandonment, but she continues to pursue love in its purest form, and that to me is priceless in a person. Shandi, you're wonderful and beautiful! Thanks for asking me the tough questions, for providing me with things to grow, and for giving me things to smile about :) oh ... and for introducing me to good, Christian rap music!

17 people like this

<u>**Comments**</u>:

☺   Hearts!

Day 7:
Portrait of a
Real Person

The Response

Portrait photography involves the face of the subject. Faces tell stories without any words or sounds - the lines in the face of an elderly veteran, the tears in the eyes of a widow, or the bright smile of a child from a foreign country.

Whether people decided to draw a literal portrait (which are really cool!) or upload portrait photography, the goal with this day was to truly capture a person who lives genuinely. It was another chance to bless someone with recognition of his or her authentic lifestyle; to give credit where credit is rightfully due.

deborahalexa: This is my neighbor...whom I just met a few weeks ago along with his wife. Today, I had the honor of soaking up some sun beside [him] and hearing his story. I am still in awe over it. This man has battled colon cancer for the last several years and is a walking miracle. He was initially told he had one month to live when he was diagnosed. Now, three years later, he's still living and battling cancer with the utmost, positive attitude! He lost his son at the age of 19 to a car accident. He has overcome addictions, been through a divorce, cancer, major financial loss, also suffered a bad stroke, and had to learn how to speak again! Just a true and real person with an amazing, open heart that has an incredible outlook on life, even after all the trials and tragedies he has been through. He blessed my life today by sharing his touching story. Bless his heart! Also, keep [him] in your prayers! His cancer is in remission, but not gone.

themoniebird: Where there are smiles, there are also tears. There are days that I feel confident, and days when I don't. Yet, at every high and low point, these two have been there. They're one of the few that can support and encourage me... also tell me how ridiculously crazy I am. They lift me up when I'm down, but will also pull my sometimes prideful butt back down to earth. Yes, there are times when I don't listen because I feel 'I'm the oldest and you shouldn't tell me what to do.' But over 90% of the time they're right. Sometimes we need a childlike perspective to pull us back and let us know how crazy some of the things we worry about are. My prayer is that when they get older, they remain true to themselves... and remember all the stuff they were fussing at me about lol.

shellritterr: This is a real portrait of a really incredible, humble, sweet, loving, amazing man. My dearest papa. RIP – I miss you! This portrait reminds me of my walk and how absolutely ANYTHING in this world is possible through God's grace. This man is my world. He was my light, my strength, my rock, my father, and my best friend. He is the reason I found God. There is not a single day that passes by that I don't think of him. I remember the very day he was diagnosed with cancer. I felt like I was punched in the face and the stomach. I was listening to his words, but at that very moment...I couldn't hear. Everything went fuzzy and dark...and scary. But I do remember he held my hands, hugged me, and let me cry. But only for a moment. He told me he wasn't afraid. I couldn't ever figure out how someone wouldn't be afraid to die. Anyways, three months later, I came home from a short mission's trip from Daytona. The whole way back (6 hours), I was thinking how in the WORLD I was going to tell him I got saved on the trip. I was so scared to tell him because I didn't know how he would react. I got the complete opposite reaction I was expecting. I will never forget all those tears. I don't think he expected me to say, 'Papa, I need to tell you something... I found God.' He was probably expecting me to say, 'I had a fun time on Daytona Beach with all of my amazing friends. Thank you for letting me go!' And a kiss good night. If it weren't for him, all the love he showed me, and the amazing schools he put me in... I guarantee you all, I wouldn't be here today. I could go on forever talking about this man. I miss him so much. I love him more than words.

Day 8:
My View at Work

leahmarieball:

I'm not in the office today, but if I were, my view would be something
similar with either a guitar or a piano. That's the amazing thing about
what I do – I don't really have an office. I take my work with me
everywhere. My title is Worship Director but over the years I've learned
that it is just that – a title. I used to think it defined who I am as an
individual and flaunt it to enhance my worth. But we're all worshippers.
The question is not whether we worship, the question is whom do we
worship? I'm proud to say I worship the King of kings and the Lord of
lords. He has given me the opportunity to make what I do daily what I
get to do for a living! To be responsible for the music portion of a church
service is a daunting task, but it is not impossible. In Christ I've been
considered worthy to do this. The other amazing part about it is that I
get to minister through my own personal music, which I also want to use

to connect people to Him. Ministry is not something I do for work – it's everywhere.

36 people like this.

<u>**Comments:**</u>

None.

Day 8:
My View At Work

The Response

"So what do you do?"

I've always cringed at that question because my view at work is slightly unconventional. I knew I wasn't the only one. What we do in life in reference to jobs, careers, schooling, etc. is a popular topic of discussion, especially when we're being introduced to someone for the first time. Some of us like to spice up what we do because it's so important to impress. But not everybody's nine to five is suit and tie material and those people need the social liberty to be proud of it.

Whether you're a stay at home mom, a teenager with a part-time job, or a full-time employee of a major corporation, what you do does not define you and what you do doesn't need to look like everyone else's definition of "work."

erica_m_reed: Well since I'm not currently working, I decided to return to school full-time. I've been back in school for a year now and everyday is more challenging than the next. I have no regrets in returning to school so late in life. I dropped out of college to work and raise my daughter. She's at an age where I can now concentrate on my studies and build a better life for us. It is my prayer that once I get my degree, I will continue to make some sort of positive impact on the kids' lives that I am involved with.

thebeautifulmess: I'm sure to the untrained eye it's a little hard to tell there is actually a desk here but YES this is my work space! I heard

Einstein had a messy desk. I'm just sayin'! So this is my view. A lovely picture window that on any given day plays a beautiful orchestra of squirrels, blue jays, the occasional cardinal, and your random maintenance worker. The secret thing about my view is that I NEVER thought I'd have it. I convinced myself early on that as part of my "walking out" my consequences were to never work in ministry. It just wouldn't be in the cards for me. Good thing I wasn't the One holding the deck!!

grace_rutledge: Because I am human, I constantly have to ask myself, 'Why am I working?' Works are empty if God isn't behind them. So instead of trying to do all these projects or acts of service, I think we should focus on making what actually counts. And not check off boxes on the 'Good Christian' list, but work only to bring God glory, no matter what it may be... school, dance, friendships, projects, sports, music...

Day 9:
A Bad Habit

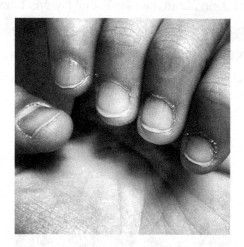

leahmarieball:

This goes beyond biting my nails, which I know is a bad habit for most people. I don't bite my nails for nothing – I've had them long before and I love them! It has nothing to do with being a guitar player either. I bite them when I'm worried, anxious, feeling out of control, upset/sad, or feeling lonely. Bad habits are indications of something that's inwardly eating away at us (pun definitely intended). And I'm not ok with that.

14 people like this

Comments:

☺   My bad habit too.

Day 9:
A Bad Habit

The Response

Everybody has at least one bad habit and they're typically formulated early on in childhood. The funny thing about bad habits is that they're never what they seem on the surface. Biting your nails or constantly tapping your foot may seem like the actual bad habit, but it's only a product of the real thing. Just like an iceberg, you have to go down deeper in order to see the bigger picture.

dsaxon15: My bad habit would be poor time management. I commit to too many things and then struggle to get them all done. This isn't good because it makes the work I do less than excellent and weakens my word. I'm better than I used to be, but I've still got a long way to go on this one.

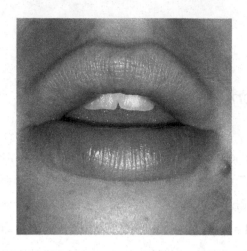

moli_mama_jay: Wanting to be [REAL], I decided against using what I assumed was a bad habit, like not putting my clothes away, or never sorting socks, and asked my husband what really makes him bonkers that I do. Apparently, I don't just apologize. I am an, "I'm sorry, but…" person. For that, I simply just say, "I'm sorry."

confidentuseofjenn: I could probably lay in bed for days and not be bothered. My bad habit is lying in bed when I should be doing anything else.

Day 10:
A Weakness

leahmarieball:

"Do not fear perfection, for you will never attain it." – Anonymous.

Perfection cannot be reached this side of heaven; there is only one Perfect
One. A strong desire that I have is not just to do well and be well in life,
but also to do the best and be the best in life. I've heard most people say
that's what we should strive for, but that's utterly exhausting and takes
the focus off of Christ. It's not "I can do all things. End of discussion" but
rather, "I can do all things through Christ." Living life with a perfectionist
mindset or viewpoint can be deadly – it zaps you of physical energy and
drains the beauty from the blessed life you're living. This is a cross I take
up daily because I don't want to continue seeing myself as valueless
because I "never measure up." My worth isn't calculated by a standard I

foolishly set, it has been established by a price I could never pay that was already paid for me.

26 people like this

<u>**Comments**</u>:

None

Day 10:
A Weakness

The Response

Weaknesses are funny things. Like bad habits, we've begun to accept them as a part of our chemistry and blame it on our background, genetics, experiences, etc. But we've got to learn to take responsibility for the things that overpower us. We've got to take control over these things and say, "Enough is enough."

caitbait77: A weakness of mine would have to be the party "lifestyle" per say. Throughout all of high school, I was always going out and doing something stupid or getting crazy. But about a year ago, I was delivered from those ways. But honestly I've back-tracked more than once since then, and that's because when you're so used to something and you just get so accustomed to it, you're "comfortable in your sin." It's still a struggle to stay away from that kind of scene, and I think it's still ok to go out and have fun, but you just have to know your limits and know when to say

enough is enough. And I'm at a good place right now where I know when enough is enough…

anonymous: It's no secret to anyone who knows me that I love tattoos and piercings. Probably more than my mother would like, actually. I currently have 10 tattoos, ears are gauged, and tongue is pierced (which is coming out very soon). I got my first tattoo when I was about 20 years old and it has been downhill since. Truth be told, if I could afford more, I'd probably be covered. Everyone who knows me knows that I love tattoos, but no one knows why I started. It wasn't because it was cool. It was a way to self-inflict pain in order to drown out the internal pain and anguish I had inside. I've struggled with depression, anger, and anxiety for as long as I can remember and never properly learned how to deal with it. I used pain as an escape. Every tattoo has some sort of significant meaning. It was during a dark period of my life.

Benjamin_james: Taking on everything at once. Sometimes I feel like there is so little time and everything needs to get done as soon as possible. But it's nice to just take a second and pay attention to those around me, especially myself. Being worn out is no way to live life.

Day II:
"Lip Service" —
What I Fail to Do

leahmarieball:

What I fail to do – follow through. Ever heard the quote, "Dreams without action are daydreams"? Most of mine turn into that. I know that we can't always do every little thing that pops into our minds, and sometimes we shouldn't. We have to have a balance and strive to maintain it. But there are some things that I truly feel compelled by God to do and never see them through. There are books I want to write, groups I want to start, songs I want to record, etc. I get distracted or discouraged mostly. I'm too busy paying attention to little road block signs like these when I need to adopt tunnel vision and keep on running. The second mile is ALWAYS the hardest, but if you push through, that second wind will carry you on.

16 people like this

Comments:

None.

Day II:
"Lip Service" –
What I Fail to Do

The Response

How many of us can relate to "all talk, no walk"? The reality is our excuses limit our ability to walk until our muscles become underworked and we end up paralyzed. Eventually we give up on our dreams because we're stuck and too far-gone to even try. "I'll do it tomorrow..." is the first enemy we have to defeat.

hannnah_leighh: From when I was a kid up until before my first mission trip this summer, I had a hard time appreciating what I have! I always wanted what other people had that I didn't! But when I went to the [Dominican Republic] this summer, it really hit me, "I NEED TO APPRECIATE WHAT I HAVE." The people that we met down there didn't have half of what I had. Now I really don't fail at appreciating. I also don't ask for many things either.

wewontnumbthepain: Yes, I know the caption and picture do not match. I am in a creative rut at the moment. I had to [research lip service] to find out what it means. It basically means hypocrisy. I think my "lip service" is gossiping. At school I think to myself all the time, 'You shouldn't be talking about that person. That's not nice. Aren't they your friends?' But honestly, I'm just as bad as everyone else with it. I will join in on gossiping conversations just so I don't feel as lonely and feel part of the group. Then, I give myself a face palm haha. Gossiping is stupid, because it's not doing any good, it's just hurting people. I've gotten A LOT better over the years, but I still struggle with it sometimes.

Julia.mariie: I say one thing and never go through with it. But, one thing I do this with constantly is saying I'll be more responsible. I say I'm going to focus on all my responsibilities like school and my friends and all those kinds of things but then something always gets in the way. I have a problem with letting things get in my way and that's something I'm definitely going to work on in 2015. No more saying one thing and doing another. I'm going to focus on getting things done when I say I'm going to get them done.

Day 12:
My Love Language

leahmarieball:

Girls love hearing "You're beautiful," but I'd rather FEEL beautiful. Ever
since I was little, I enjoyed being hugged, tickled, snuggled, kissed,
and cuddled. Ask anyone in my family. I love words but there's nothing
like contact with someone you love and trust. I've seen this aspect in
relationships distorted and abused, but thanks to the Lord's grace, I'm
hopeful for restoration. He makes all things new. He is the Author of love
and affection, intimacy, and dare I type ... sex. It's true. In His hands, we
are always made to FEEL love.

37 people like this

Comments:

☺   PJ!*

* The hand I'm holding in the picture is my little brother, PJ.

Day 12:
My Love Language

The Response

If you've never heard the term "love language," it's ok; not many people have. There are five: 1) physical touch, 2) words of affirmation, 3) acts of service, 4) quality time, and 5) giving gifts. You can take an assessment online to learn about your love language.

There seems to be some reverse psychology that goes on when it comes to making love languages fluent in our lives. The best way to show love is by learning the other person's language, not by going off of your own. This is truly selfless, the best way to love.

renddslow: Physical Touch. Be it a pat on the back, a hug, or a kiss. Oh, and getting my back rubbed, that's my favorite…

simply_hannah94: Quality time, that is my love language. Spending time with friends and family is how I communicate.

cyergs92: To be honest, I had no idea what this was. I looked it up and realized there are five love languages: words of affirmation, quality time, physical touch, gift giving, and acts of service. These are the 5 ways that make people feel most loved and everyone has their own major one. I took a quiz and wasn't surprised that I got words of affirmation and quality time as a strong number 2. When people encourage me through their words,

say they're proud of me, or even compliment me on how I look that day it really makes me feel loved. I also love spending time with the people I love by going on adventures or simply [watching movies]. This has helped me understand myself a little more and highly advise you take this quiz too!

Day 13:
An Addiction [PAST]

leahmarieball:

Regardless that this is a past addiction, it isn't easy to put out there; however, it's the only thing I was hooked on. From the age of 10 to the age of 15, I was addicted to pornography. It started in my friend's bedroom late one night when her parents were asleep. They had cable in the house ... What was supposed to be a fun sleepover turned into twisted images on her TV. None of us knew what we were looking at, much less, getting ourselves involved in. That started a downward spiral into a place of darkness that is difficult to describe. It eventually led me into depression and isolation. Those images haunted me and caused me to question love, sex, and my own self-image - "What's wrong with me?" Thankfully, with support and help from my parents and a few wise mentors at church, God delivered me out of that pit. It's a vicious monster that doesn't just tear at your own heart; it injures those around you. Men and women alike are affected, but those of us in the church have become so silent about this sin that people are embarrassed to speak up. It *is* humiliating, which is why I will not joke about it, take it lightly, or throw daggers at those who struggle with it. It's a silent killer, and I've been there. But I'm out. "Who the Son sets free is free indeed."

46 people like this

Comments:

☺   Thank you. It's almost impossible for men to speak about it and you're the first woman I've seen that's been bold enough to call out what God has saved you from. Seriously proud of you.

☺   Thank you for posting this, Leah! You are awesome and I am so proud of you.

☺   You are just so awesome. I'm so proud to call you a close friend.

☺   #realtalk

☺   And this is how we show who Jesus is ... love you girl.

☺   Love you girl! This is so awesome!

☺   #yourock

☺   #powpow

☺   You are so bold and honest for sharing this with us. God is smiling at you and how amazing you are for stepping out and showing how He has won those battles we have all struggled with!

☺   #danggirl #YouAreAwesomeGirl

☺   You are such an inspiration. I know it couldn't have been easy to put this out there. Your honesty is admirable.

☺   ...You have guts girl. To socially admit the struggle that can so often hold us in bondage to fear, shame, and defeat is deeply commendable. I applaud you for your step of bravery, and rejoice with you in freedom.

Day 13:
An Addiction [PAST]

The Response

Addiction is a crippling word. It's isolating too. Public enemy #1: ourselves. Trust me, I've been there. It's hard to silence the condemning voices inside one's mind.

When I dared to be real about my past addiction, the only voices coming back at me were encouraging and uplifting. The same happened for many people as they revealed secrets of the past - depression, cutting, suicide, eating disorders, pornography, and much more. The response to their honesty was so hopeful.

mrskayallen: No matter how many times you hear the words "You're so skinny," it's often heard and never believed. I'm sure I'm not the only girl who has ever struggled with this. Ever since middle school, I have been obsessed or addicted to weight maintenance. I'd do whatever it took to make sure my waistline was as small as it could be. I guess in a way I was addicted to physical perfection. Whether it meant skipping a few meals, depriving myself of sleep, and pushing myself to the point of unbearable hunger. No matter how many times I looked in the mirror, I always noticed something I needed to change, one more pound I could lose. I didn't believe God did a good enough job, so I was going to do everything I could to make it what I thought it should have been. What God brought me out of was a pit that I could have never gotten out of on my own. He took the tears of repentance and replaced them with His joy and healing. There is power in the Name of Jesus. He will break every chain.

kleechristine: My addiction wasn't anything drastic on the surface, because the damage it did wasn't noticeable on the surface. All throughout high school, I was addicted to romance novels. Not the weird ones that look blatantly inappropriate, but stuff like "The Notebook" and all those other Nicholas Sparks books. It was something I didn't realize how bad it really was until God got me out of it. It created unrealistic expectations in my head of relationships and myself. I battled with a lot of lustful thoughts and negative mindsets. But because of God's amazing love being lavished on this little heart of mine, He has taken what Satan meant for my destruction and redeemed it. He has reminded me that my beauty is for Him and from Him. He has restored me.

anonymous: Here's God's redemption story. I'm not afraid to say it, but I was addicted to porn a few years back. It was prior to me being a strong believer, and it was by far the hardest fight of my life. It took me a long time to overcome, but I made it. Now because of that addiction, I have respect for [the types of] girls [that] guys so much lack these days. God has replaced me with new eyes, which are set straight on my mission.

anonymous: I started lying first to get me out of situations that were overly controlling. If I told the truth about anything, I was then demanded to explain farther than I could and made to feel bad about anything I ever said or did, even if there wasn't anything wrong with what I said or did. It was a very strange type of emotional abuse. I made a decision that if I lied, then I wouldn't be made to feel as bad. I was right. I started lying about small things. I would get a thrill out of the feeling of finally being able to run my own life. I was the only one that really knew what was going on. Then my small lies grew into bigger lies, my bigger lies into cover-ups, and my cover-ups into about six different lives I had to live. I had the control now, and I loved it. At the climax of this chapter of my life, I had one life I lived at work, one I lived at school, one I lived at home, one that I lived with my boyfriend that my parents didn't know about, one that I lived with my friends that knew about my secret boyfriend, and one that I lived with my friends that didn't know about my secret boyfriend. I started lying out of habit. When asked a question, I would begin to think up a response that would check out with whatever stories I had told that particular person. I had gotten myself into a place where I needed to lie and had become pretty good at it considering everything I needed to keep up with. When truths finally did begin to come out, I saw how I hurt and lost the trust of the people I loved the most. I did a lot of praying, crying, and truth telling during this time. I prayed that hearts that used to be controlling would no longer be controlling, so that I didn't feel the need to lie anymore. I cried to those I had hurt to forgive me and trust me and I told those who were involved truths that had been covered so long with lies. With God's grace and mercy and the passing of time and truths exposed, I can now stand as somebody that does not feel the need or desire to lie to anyone about things in my life. I can, however, spot a liar with little trying.

Day 14:
An Addiction
[PRESENT]

leahmarieball:

This was a tough one because I have a few current addictions. But the more crippling addiction I have at the present is justice… my own distorted version of justice. I'm addicted to seeing cruel, heartless, thoughtless, manipulative, and selfish people punished or made to taste their own poison. It hurts my heart when it seems like these people "get off" and live their lives in such a happy, fulfilling manner. I know that as Christians we are called to forgive because the unforgiveable has been forgiven in us, but I get so incredibly angry with God when it seems like the offender offers a simple "Sorry," and walks away unscathed. This is very sensitive to me (just being REAL… I'm actually crying as I type this out haha), because recently I've been deeply wounded by two individuals and left to bandage my wounds while they prosper. I know, I know – you probably have a plethora of Scripture to throw my way in the comment section ☺ haha I won't reject them. But understand that I know what the Word says. In my humanness and imperfection, I'm admitting to portions of the Bible I find difficult to swallow, but I do not deny them. It's ok to argue with God or be honest with Him. In fact He welcomes it. Everyday, I'm going to pray, "Lord, give me compassion for people as You heal my wounds and make me whole again. I release these people into Your capable and loving hands." Maybe you've been there or are there. I'm with you on this ((hugs)).

37 people like this

Comments:

☺   This is why Psalms is my favorite book. It is a beautiful thing to know that we are not the only ones who throw temper tantrums at the Lord sometimes… all because we are hurting. Totally with you on this one.

☺   I'm actually right there too. I get so frustrated when my version of justice isn't fulfilled. I don't always think of what God is up to because I can't see it. I see the here and the now and right here, right now, this person needs to be punished for what they have done. I have to remember my own sin, all the ways that I should be punished. I pray often and hard for eyes to see like Jesus, to be able to see the outcome.

Day 14:
An Addiction
[PRESENT]

The Response

Even harder than PAST addictions are those monsters we still battle every day. This day of the challenge took more than guts. This day was all about grabbing the demons head-on and wrestling them to the ground. This day was more than just confession, but the first step towards freedom and healing.

anonymous: I think about sex a lot. I used to have sex a lot. I had many awkward situations because of sex. I have made stupid decisions because of sex. I have been sexually assaulted because of my laid-back approach to sex. I have cried over boys many times because I have tried to force love with sex. I have ruined close friendships with sex. I have endangered my health and my future because of sex. I have encountered things and done things that I would never admit in public even if I were being real because of sex. I have personally experienced most of the negative repercussions with sex before marriage and sex before love. I made a decision a few weeks ago. I'm taking it back. I'm not giving in anymore. I'm putting up physical and mental boundaries and I WILL stick to them. I WILL expect my future boyfriend to stick to them. I WILL refuse to compromise. I'm kept awake at night, my mind racing, tears flowing, wishing I could go back and erase parts of my past and just make it right, hating myself for the things I've done. I picture what my life could be if I knew then what I know now, if I could undo the mistakes. It is so incredibly hard to forgive myself. Will I ever make it right? I don't know how to fix this. But maybe I'm not meant to be the one to fix it. Maybe I'm the one meant to be fixed.

rad_rebekah: My present addiction is anxiety. I tend to worry about a lot of things that aren't really worth worrying about. This has become such a bad addiction or habit of doing that I end up in tears because I overwhelm myself so much. I get so worried that I can't enjoy what's happening now because I'm so worried about something that might (probably won't) happen days ahead.

rebekahcbaines: Story lines. Wait… what? Something or some things I'm currently addicted to. If I'm watching a movie or TV show or reading a book, I can't put it down or turn it off till I know the end of the story!

Day 15:
A Regret

leahmarieball:

I have only one regret. Everything else in my life has been a stepping-stone to get where I am today; a circumstance that's made me stronger, refined my character, and added to my testimony. But there is one I'm learning to let go of - past sexual sin. If I were honest … this "good, Christian" girl has done anything and everything. It's just as difficult to type because it's there before me in black and white. I don't regret relationships or the guys I grew to know; I've learned something valuable from each one. I regret rejecting Godly counsel. I regret ignoring the Lord's guidance and waiting on Him. I regret indifferent compliance. I regret allowing myself to be put in compromising situations. All of this adds up to the one regret that haunts me - giving pieces of myself away. It's not a game and it's not "having fun." I don't care what the world says. There is nothing more beautiful than a woman who keeps herself pure and her heart guarded. It is a priceless treasure for her future husband. For me it's hard to look into the future and see myself that way. But I'm moving forward trusting that God, who is able to give sight to the blind, heal the sick, and raise the dead, can surely redeem my dirty past.

31 people like this

<u>Comments:</u>

☺   #powerful

☺   I'm grateful to call you my friend.

☺   You are precious. Never forget that.

☺   Powerful transparency. Proud of you.

Day 15:
A Regret

The Response

Ok … I want to challenge your thinking with this statement: it's OK to have regrets.

Regret is defined as "a sense of loss, disappointment, dissatisfaction; to show sorrow or remorse over an act or a fault." For years I told myself, "I have NO regrets" because of that familiar phrase, "Live life with no regrets." Did of any of us stop and think what that truly meant? It means, live life with no sorrow or remorse over things you've done wrong, don't ever experience disappointment, dissatisfaction, and don't get upset when you lose someone or something you love. Just don't. Because otherwise you're not really living.

Wait … what!? I've retired that phrase for myself.

Regrets aren't bad. It's our response to regret that can cause us to live in a defeated state of mind. But regret itself causes us to analyze, evaluate, consider, and observe the portions of our lives where we messed up, where we could have but we didn't, where we let go when we shouldn't have. Even things that are out of our control, it's ok to experience regret. Let that sorrow out or it will eat you from the inside. But then, move on. Use your regret to learn, to reevaluate, and to teach others.

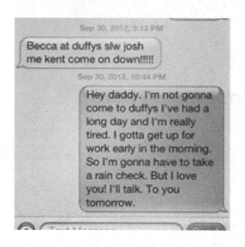

beccadempsey: In life we are often asked, "What is your one regret? What do you wish you could have done?" For most of my life it was always a shallow answer of 'I wish I would have played this sport' or 'tried harder in math class' – things that I thought were important. On September 30th, 2012, the whole course of my life changed. Not from a class I didn't pass or a sport I didn't try out for, but because my dad, my best friend, was in a motorcycle accident. That night was the last night I would speak to my dad again. If only I had known that just four hours after telling him I couldn't come see him because I was tired, I would get a knock on my door that would change everything. The next two weeks I spent watching my dad, the strongest man I know, lay lifeless in a bed. The only response I ever got was the squeeze of my hand. No matter how much I tried to talk to him, yell at him, and cry over him, he never woke up. Yes this is my biggest regret. Not taking time out of my life for my dad, the man who always gave himself up for me. Somehow though this regret is made easier knowing that my dad may be gone for now, but not forever. With the constant reminder that God has a purpose that I may not see or understand, but I know He is guiding me along the way. His grace, mercy, and strength are what are getting me through each day. Looking to Him for unending joy and not the things that are here but for a moment.

curioushobbit: I'm a big advocate for this now, but a regret I have/had would be not coming out of my shell and meeting/getting to know people – even through my freshmen year of college I was like this. But since then, a lot of growth has happened. The Lord taught me to stay put and to lean in. For one I think it would've been straight-physically impossible. Two, definitely mentally impossibly. Three, that friendships like these are calling me to live better and be better and grow up into the person I am. Sometimes all we can do is stay put, show up, lean in, and give our best. I'm learning.

anonymous: Obviously, I'm human, so I have my fair share of regrets. One of my biggest though is what happened a couple of years ago. I was at one of the darkest times of my life, where I was just continually hurting myself, emotionally and physically. I tried to hide my problems through worry and denial, but in the end, it just exploded them. I'm proud to say that I fought through everyday and learned healthy ways to live my life. I will never get that time back. I wasted so much of my life on worry and that is something I'll always regret, but have accepted.

Day 16:
A Family Member
I Admire

leahmarieball:

My dad. Let's be honest - if you saw how long this could be with all the things I could say about my dad, you wouldn't read it. I couldn't fill a Facebook status, and 140 characters on Twitter wouldn't cut it. There's no need to put anything through a filter when it comes to this man. I'm not being lazy. My dad is the most incredible man I've ever met. I've lived my life striving to please him, not because he would love me more, but because his approval matters. Wisdom, strength, godliness, integrity, courage, sacrifice, faithfulness, determination, and undeniable mercy - these are only some of the things that make up his character. I love him very much.

37 people like this

Comments:

☺   He was a stud back in the day! #ihopethisisntawkward

☺   Hasn't changed a bit! Definitely on my list of men I would like my son to model himself after.

Day 16:
A Family Member
I Admire

The Response

Family is vital. What other human relationship in our lifetime is replicated in successful business and church models? The "family" element is what determines return business or turns visitors into regular attenders. It's because family is about belonging, acceptance, and nurturing that we wouldn't otherwise find.

In our own families, it can be hard to pick just one person that we admire. But maybe we only have one person left to choose from, or maybe our family looks like a small group or an adopted family unit. Whatever it looks like, the elements are still the same. Those that we admire within that unit have helped to shape us into the people we are today, and that deserves recognition.

kristi_alena19: Well, I couldn't decide on one obviously, but let me tell yah, my parents are truly some of the GREATEST people you will meet in your life. My parents have the biggest hearts for the youth. Growing up, my parents were high school leaders for at least seven years. They welcomed plenty of youth into our house over the years, just loving on them. Watching how my parents love people has been truly amazing. But recently, I admire and respect my parents on a whole new level, as the last month and a half have not been very normal for us. My dad got sick and was hospitalized for over a week, but … just because my dad got sick doesn't mean he stopped praising God or that he blamed God. To watch him worship God, it is music to my ears and just something that lifts my spirits. If my father, who is dealing with daily pain, does this and worships with his whole heart, why can't I do the same? My mother … I totally respect her and what she's doing for my family. To watch her husband suffer isn't a fun thing to do but she keeps her head up and pushes through. I love them both so much and am thankful they are my parents.

djjazzypoov: In my family, it's impossible to choose just one. My parents are extraordinary. They've shown me what unconditional, selfless love really looks like every day of my life. And my brothers are the coolest, smartest, funniest guys I know, and so full of kindness, compassion, and strength. Plus, we all actually like each other and get along. We're friends. It's kinda amazing. I'm blessed right outta my socks.

Madi_marie_97: I can't think of any better admiration than my parents. They are role models through their lifestyles, in their faith, in their love and commitment, to us and each other, and by their humble, servant-like attitudes. SO blessed to have them.

Day 17:
A Transformation

leahmarieball:

Africa was never on my agenda, so neither were the people. I would pray or give an offering but selfishly declined any other method of getting involved, masking it with the excuse of going elsewhere to serve. "Everyone goes to Africa." Well, I soon discovered why that's the case. If God sends you, you'll go His way or the rough way! After I went, my eyes weren't opened; my heart burst open. I was completely transformed by this experience. God used two amazing little boys to rock my cold-hearted world. I would do anything even die for these kids. They mean the world to me, so I know they mean more to Him. And He allowed me to go. Crazy. I'm not the same because of Kenya.

35 people like this

Comments:

☺   Stinkin' love those little smiles!

Day 17:
A Transformation

The Response

There are these trends on Instagram that people have adopted -
"Throwback Thursday," "Flashback Friday," and "Transformation Tuesday."
Transformation - what a beautiful word. A change … a shift … an
alteration, completely miraculous in and of itself, especially when it comes
to people.

When people are transformed, whether in a positive or negative way,
other people notice. "What has happened to you?" There's something
undeniably different. Not just different in a way that effects the individual's
life, but different in a way that's contagious. It spreads. It catches. People
are impacted. When we are open about the transformations that have taken
place in our lives, when we're willing to share them with other people, it
spreads. It catches. Hope is transferred from one body to the next.

anonymous: 10 months ago, I was in the best shape of my life. I was in the gym on a day-to-day basis, 138 lbs. and 14% body fat. I was lifting heavy and I was healthy and fit. Nine months ago, I got super sick and was later diagnosed with Lyme disease. I couldn't do the thing I enjoyed the most (the gym). I couldn't do school, I couldn't do much of anything. I was always fatigued and weak, I was losing my hearing, the grip in my hands, blacking out, and I always had these stabbing pains in my head. I had these intense pains in my back, causing me not to move, and I weighed 178 lbs. All of these things messed with me. I went crazy, I hated myself; I just wanted all of this pain to be over. I found myself in my bathroom, with a knife to my wrist, depressed. This disease ruined my life. I lost everything I cared about, but where one door closes, another door opens. I'm still trying to find that door. I know that God is going to use this as a testimony, and I just want to give everybody a HUGE thank you that never left my side and prayed for me and stuck by me as I went through this rough patch. (P.S. I'm feeling a whole lot better now. Still on meds, but a lot better! I can do almost everything I used to do, just not too much activity.)

sadiemae2013: From being awkward and nerdy to still being awkward and nerdy.

kaitlyn__churchill: Wow, freshman to senior year. It may only look like a few little physical changes, but that's only the surface. Band has changed my life and me as a person in ways I can't even begin to express.

Day 18:
Something I
Grieve Over

leahmarieball:

The results of cyber bullying: depression, isolation, eating disorders, self-mutilation, and suicide. It makes me sick to read how people who are called "friends" on social media lash out at each other because of something they disagree over. I hating logging online to read an article only to get to the comment section to see people passionately involved in arguments that are unrelated to the above article, but somehow, following a trail of disagreements, you find where everything broke loose. Why does such an intelligent, dominant species – the human race – insist on engaging in one of the most disgraceful, foolish, unethical, and weak approaches as this, all for the sake of being right... of appearing stronger... wiser ... prettier ... better... because we're scared of what we read or see, or are intimidated by it? So our first reaction is to attack? It sickens me. I grieve for the families of those whose children have taken their lives because they decided that death was easier than dealing with the world's constant criticism. It's a huge reason why [REAL] exists.

37 people like this

Comments:

☺   So much yes!

Day 18:
Something I
Grieve Over

The Response

Life. It isn't fair. Thanks for the reminder, right? We've all experienced it to some extent. But I wonder if it happens more often than we'd like because our definition of "fair" is distorted. It's not about what's truly just, but what works for us, on our time, in our way, and whatever is most beneficial for our well-being.

There comes a point where we need to take responsibility for our selfishness ... our pride ... our own mistakes. We need to realize that the decisions we make in this life don't just affect our future, but also affect the future of those around us. Because of the broken world we live in - an "every man for himself" type of mindset - there is injustice, pain, sickness, deception, and much more. Evil is present. And we grieve. But just like regret, grief can be used to challenge us, motivate us to action, and bring awareness to real issues that deserve a voice.

djjazzypoov: Orphans. The fact that there are millions of children in the world without mommies and daddies to hug them and tuck them in at night, who end each day hungry, scared, and alone. That thousands upon thousands of American children are wasting away in a broken foster system because no one wants them, while couples line up by the hundreds for an "unscathed-newborn." This rips my heart right out of my chest and makes me cry every time I think about it. This is why my husband and I are deeply called to adopt our children. If JESUS said that the only true religion is to care for orphans and widows in their distress (and He did), perhaps the church needs to take that more seriously. Christians outnumber orphans 7 to 1. This is a crisis that wouldn't exist if the church would just BE THE CHURCH and do something about it.

lizzyyybee: The thought of not being able to remember the things that I tend to take for granted makes me sad. I want to remember everything. Like the way my grandfather laughs, and how my brother leaves trash everywhere and how it annoys me but he makes me laugh, so it's alright. I want to be able to remember how it feels to wake up after it has snowed, and I'm able to sleep in and not have to go to school. I want to remember people's names. I want to remember the story that the cashier told me just in case we meet again, so I can tell her I remember (maybe it will make her smile, or it will creep her out, but I won't mind because I remembered). I want to remember the feeling I get when I just know my mom is home from work, even before we see each other. I want to remember the way my grandma looks when she's playing piano. I want to remember all of it, and I know I probably won't. So as of right now I'm going to live day by day and lock these memories up, so that just maybe I'll be able to open them again one day.

gabsaimee: Child abuse. In any form, verbally or physically. It hurts and damages in ways we can't even imagine. Whenever I see or hear about a kid being abused, my heart aches. If I could have a superpower, it would be the power of being present whenever a child is about to be hurt, so I can stop it and make his [or her] life better. Kids are kids - they are meant to be protected and loved. They don't know the way, we must show it to them. They are not an object in which we can vent our anger and frustration.

Day 19:
A Walk in
My Shoes

leahmarieball:

I own 14 pairs of high heels, seven pairs of boots, 11 pairs of sandals,
11 pairs of flats, and seven pairs of sneakers. Just being honest. You're
welcome to borrow any, but my feet are rather large. I think that's why
I like this pair of sneakers so much. They were only $10 and they're
so comfortable. Plus they just fit *me*. As I've gotten older, I've enjoyed
dressing up more and more, but I'll always have a spot on me that tells the
story of my "Tom-boy" days. Give me a pair of shoes I can run in or easily
climb a tree and I'm golden. Again, I'm not opposed to dressier options but
the sporty side eventually comes out.

31 people like this

Comments:

☺ The running bug is in us! I always feel safer/more comfortable in a pair of sneakers I can run in. We will be in our 90's and you, Ash and I will still be out there running. A little slower, but hey, who cares about personal records then??

☺ Nah ladies. At 90 it's all about water aerobics so that we stay upright.

☺ Sweet shoes.

☺ I might do this challenge!

Day 19:
A Walk in
My Shoes

The Response

Guys and girls alike really get into shoes. They aren't just for practical purposes - they are a literal walking picture of who we are. Don't be fooled by the expensive Nike pair or the designer peep-toe heels. Many people have their "go-to" pair where they let go and let themselves be themselves for a while. Anything that is comfortable, looks good, and let's us live life the way we like it ... those are some good shoes.

therealcorysullivan: So I don't know if this is normal, but for a guy, I have lots of shoes. I have boots, about 6 pairs of converse, a couple pairs of dress shoes, a pair of black sneakers for work, and a couple pairs of running shoes. These running shoes here are not necessarily my favorite, but I would consider them my most important. Most of my life, I have struggled with my weight. And I know it's not cool for men to talk about physical attributes that they are not comfortable with, but it is what it is. Because I've struggled with my weight, my confidence has never been all that high. It started with just having low confidence with women, but it has leaked into other facets of my life. Anytime I appear to be confident, it's usually just a mask to disguise the insecurity that just wants to jump out and hide in a corner lol. So here's what I've done through my life. I've lost weight on and off and gained some muscle in hoping to gain confidence. That didn't work. I bought new clothes so that I might have more confidence. That didn't work. Tried different hairstyles, got contacts, did whatever I felt like I had to trying to look better, whatever "better" actually is, and none of it has ever worked. Here's what I came to realize a few years ago. You cannot change something externally and think that the internal is just going to follow suit. Because this insecurity is not merely an external issue. It's a heart problem. And I can't change that. But Jesus can. By giving my life to Christ, he took all that insecurity and nailed it to a cross, and so now as I love my life, I can't boast in myself, but instead I boast in God who has started a good work in me and has promised through the Bible to bring the work He has started to completion. So now these particular shoes remind me every time I work out and go running that my life isn't about me and my insecurities but instead is about God and all He has done to bring those insecurities to an end, which means that my working out is no longer in vain, but is about my physical body in a state of health that will allow me to be used by God for whatever He has called me to for as long as I live.

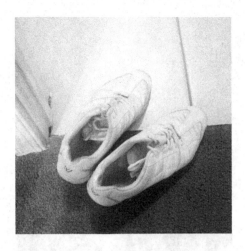

jules_mirita: For anyone who doesn't know, these are my Varsity's. Although I have "prettier" shoes these are by far my favorite pair. These shoes represent something that has become such a blessing in my life: cheer. When I was sick, cheer was such a great distraction and didn't allow me to think about it and something to look forward to. Two years later and it has become something I love and am so thankful to be apart of. I absolutely love all of the girls I have been given the opportunity to cheer with and the family they have become to me. These shoes act as a reminder of the sport I love and the family of amazing girls and coaches that I have acquired throughout it.

Day 20:
What Inspires Me

leahmarieball:

I met a guy named [John] last year who completely surrendered his life to the Lord after almost 20 years of battling drugs, alcohol, and sexual sin. People see his tattoos and piercings, but God pointed out his kind heart and gracious smile. He dug down into the Word and asked hard questions. Two years ago I met [Melissa] - a beautiful, free-spirited young woman who was always smiling when she entered church. She joined a Bible study I was leading and refused to just accept things that people said just because we were inside a church building. I have a friend named [Katie] who has developed a type of strength I rarely see in girls her age because of the events that have transpired in her lifetime. She stumbles but doesn't stay down. She has taught me how to be real and keep going. What inspires me?? The "underdogs" - those people outside that we often overlook, ignore, or immediately judge because of their reputation. However, let God get a hold of these people, and they fling themselves full force into His grace because it's the sweetest thing they've ever known.

They're real people who want to be loved, and continue to pursue Christ in the midst of their humanity. I'm inspired by their strength and childlike faith.

38 people like this

<u>**Comments:**</u>

None.

Day 20:
What Inspires Me

The Response

Inspiration doesn't just appear. The very definition contains words like "fill", "pour", and "arouse." There has to be something pulling the trigger. We can definitely turn to music or a serene mountaintop scene. But inspiration isn't truly useful unless it triggers action.

We can be truly passionate about something but lack the maturity to follow-through and utilize that passion to change the course of history. The hardest step to take is the second step. Reminding yourself why you started - going back to the source of that inspiration - raises the bar on the action to follow.

cassisberriess: STORIES. I love stories – people's stories of God's faithfulness, people's stories of God's healing and people walking in faith…a story I just heard yesterday of a friend ministering to a bunch of punk teenagers through her kindness to a drunk man! I was floored by her actions. Stories are great ☺

renddslow: People who travel the world and make a difference. I watched this…talk once by a guy who went all over the world talking to dangerous people about having one day of peace. And another guy in a short sermon talked about going into communist occupied Cuba to preach the Gospel. And honestly nothing inspires me more.

racheljanethree: The Bible. My main source of inspiration. Nothing else is stable in this world, but one thing I can always count on is God. His Word is always real and true and I can count on Him for everything I need.

Day 21:
First Thought in
the Morning

leahmarieball:

Time always seems to be on my mind, even first thing in the morning. My alarm goes off, and even though I'm "slow to rise," I still lay back and think, "I have to get up because I have this much time to do this and this and ... " You might think, well why do you lie there? As crazy as it seems, sometimes just thinking of all the things I need to accomplish paralyzes me and I feel safer in one spot. I know that's unrealistic, but it's the truth. This morning though, and for the past few weeks, the Lord in His grace has been waking me up and saying, "Let's talk first..." And that always ends up changing my entire viewpoint.

34 people like this

Comments:

☺ Gosh, this picture would look better with a certain ... white watch. Hahahaha!

☺ Beautiful perspective. I love this.

☺ That watch. Mmmm!

☺ [Awesome] watch, girl!

Day 21:
First Thought
in the Morning

The Response

My brain isn't fully functioning in the morning until the first few sips of coffee. Sure enough, I discovered many people wake up with the same kind of feelings or emotions. And that's ok.

It's nice to know you're not the only one wishing you could hit "snooze" just one more time. But there are some people who wake with regrets … wake up with fear … wake up feeling nothing at all. I think the most important thing for us to do is get into the habit of waking up THANKFUL. Waking up in a spirit of gratefulness determines the rest of your day.

invisiblecheers: Lately, my first thought has been**,** "Why am I awake?" or "What do I have to do today?" Lately I've been feeling pretty down and kind of like my brain isn't totally there. I've been slowly coming out of it, but it's still pretty hard to get up in the morning. Being able to talk about my… whatever you want to call it, has been very helpful in bringing me back to Earth.

simply_hannah94: My first thought in the morning on most days is "Cat, get off of me!" "Why do I have to get up?" And/or "Where is the coffee?"

rad_Rebekah: Coffee time.

Day 22:
Favorite Scripture,
Quote, or Lyric

WE ARE
not perfect human beings,
NOR DO WE HAVE TO
pretend to be,
BUT IT is necessary
FOR US TO BE THE
best version of ourselves
WE CAN BE.

leahmarieball:

Anything that relates to authenticity or identity catches my attention. I can't choose just one, like I can't choose just one verse in the Bible that gets me. Whoever said this, bravo.

46 people like this

Comments:

☺   But you are perfect Mrs. Almost Young.

Day 22:
Favorite Scripture,
Quote, or Lyric

The Response

Music inspires us and gets inside of us, not because of the melody alone, but because of the lyrics. Quotes surface all over social media. Scripture is used for religious and secular purposes alike. It's a favorite for a reason and usually it's due to the sentimental value. These words found us crying on our bedroom floor or gave us the courage to open up our mouth and speak.

Scripture speaks. The Bible says, "The Word of God is living and active…" (Hebrews 4:12). When God speaks, things happen. The words you read in the Bible are not just words, or quotes, or online memes. They should never be taken lightly.

Curioushobbit: Well, I have a lot of all of those actually… but I decided to choose Scripture and specifically, Psalm 23:3 – ["He restores my soul. He leads me in paths of righteousness for His Name's sake."] And with all of my heart, mind, and soul, I want Him to restore me. Nothing else will do. It may not be the safest or "convenient" way to live. Carrying all these feelings for people, seeing things with a different set of eyes, and places and moments in life orchestrated by something bigger that I cannot control, but I can't imagine living, truly living, any other way.

["Remember that everyone you meet is afraid of something, loves something, and has lost something." – H. Jackson Brown, Jr.]

madi_marie_97: Ahh I can't pick one! I live off all of those... So here is the most recent one I saved. One of my favorite verses, the verse in my bio, is Philippians 1:20 – "I eagerly expect and hope that I will be in no way ashamed but will have sufficient courage so that now, as always, Christ may be exalted through my body, whether by life or by death." This is my life goal. To have courage, to be unashamed, and to glorify God through my living and through my death.

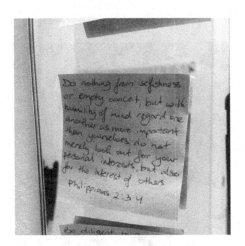

ylia.rae: I dislike self-absorbed people and constantly check myself to make sure I don't become like them. Not saying that I'm selfless at all... I could use some work. But yeah, I guess this is uncommon scripture to use as a favorite but I like it. Need that reminder sometimes.

Day 23:
OOTD – Outfit
of the Day

[When Im Staying In]

leahmarieball:

"Outfit of the day" pictures on Instagram always puzzled me because the people I saw posting these amazing outfits, with perfect hair and makeup, were the very people I knew were staying home on a Saturday. I don't know about you, but I'll admit that I don't look like that when I'm not going anywhere. This is me in my "glory" - straight bumming it. I work out, clean house, run errands ... and I look like this doing it.

39 people like this

Comments:

☺   What up muscles? Lol.

☺ I feel better about [my outfit] now … I was like … dang … maybe you need to reevaluate your life.

☺ You missed a day of your own challenge! I feel better knowing I missed a day too lol.

Day 23:
OOTD – Outfit
of the Day

The Response

Outfit of the day is another Instagram trend. Here's my issue with OOTD: how accurate are these photos? There isn't anything wrong with wanting to get dressed up and show it off. It's fun. It's creative. It's expressive, but accurate? Not many of these posts are real.

We tend to forget that people plan these outfits out … they don't look like that every day when they're grocery shopping, walking the dog, cleaning the bathroom. It's like a person's "phone-voice," sweet, melodic … veiled. But behind closed doors, we lose the designer threads and opt for sweats. And that's perfectly ok.

Day 24:
A "Mirror" Pic -
Transparent Moment

leahmarieball:

Mirror pictures are all over Instagram - guys and girls alike post them.
I believe they're always intentional, even if the person's caption is "just
goofing around." How can anyone miss a mirror? It gives us exactly what
we want to see, and yet, it also gives us everything we don't want to see:
ourselves. People see the outer reflection and we are the real deal that is
often masked. I have numerous things I could be transparent about but
this one will do. Whether I come off as humble, insecure, or confident,
I struggle with pride. Insecurity is just a false sense of pride so don't be
fooled. This challenge has truly challenged me to be real, be me, be
humble, and be a woman of integrity.

30 people like this

Comments:

☺   Can you text me the 30-day REAL challenge beginning picture? I want to do it.

Day 24:
A "Mirror" Pic –
Transparent Moment

The Response

Another Instagram trend is the infamous "mirror" pic. It's self-explanatory. Find a mirror anywhere (although restrooms, especially public ones, are the popular spot) and snap a pic. Girls do these more than guys, but they're definitely not exempt.

Humans love mirrors. They show us everything we love to see - ourselves. But … they show us the surface stuff. If we spent a good few minutes staring at ourselves in the mirror, would we start to notice deeper things? Would we see the things that mirrors don't tell, the things we're terrified to see? Is this what other people see? Or have we become so skilled at pretending that it's impossible to penetrate? Like a thick layer of glass, good luck trying to crack us! But transparency is POWERFUL. Transparency teaches us to be true to our reflection, to live out our words and be the person we are, not just in private, but also for other people to see.

tnmfg: This is me 20 minutes ago. Dropping the kids off at a theatre rehearsal. I'm wearing a hat. Something I do to hide. Because right now in my life that's what I want to do. Hide. The truth of the matter is that I can't really do that. How do you hide from yourself? How do you run from disappointing others? How do you hide from a breaking heart? Especially when you think you are doing the right thing. I know I am doing the right thing. So why is that so hard? So this is me right now. Hiding. Hiding from the looks I get when I run into someone, who believes the things told about me behind my back. Hiding. Hiding my emotion, from my husband, who just wants to be told that his dad will be ok, that he will beat cancer. Hiding what I see and feel in my heart. Life is hard. We aren't promised happy endings.

rebekahcbaines: Females. Never satisfied with the way we look in the mirror. We look in the reflection and we search to find the image we want to see. We look to find the girl we want to be, we search for who we think we are supposed to be. Be satisfied with who you are and what you look like. Being confident in your God-given beauty is not being vain. Don't confuse being confident [with vanity]. You are beautiful. I am beautiful. We are beautiful because we are who He made us to be. Stop searching for another girl in the mirror; enjoy the one looking back at you.

sarah_hixon: Wanna know where I thought I would be ten years ago…? Not living [where I am today] with two friends, and [working as] a youth pastor at [my church]. I had set up huge expectations for what my life would be and have had to learn that His plans are greater than mine. Being single at 24 is ok. Having [God] reshape your dreams is ok. Enjoying the now and not worrying about the future is ok. Are there moments where I throw pity parties? Yes, all the time! I love this scripture that I have on my mirror in my room and it's one that has gotten me through many pity parties and will continue to!

Day 25:
A True Celebrity

leahmarieball:

This is Andrew (not the baby although, he's great too). Andrew is a self-employed musician and works part-time at Starbucks. He gets up during the week at four AM, goes to work, and goes home. On the weekends, he's usually traveling with the various artists he plays drums for. This man isn't "almost famous" for the physical aspects of his lifestyle, but rather what takes place inwardly. This is a man who loves the Lord, loves his family, and loves the people around him. He plays drums in ministry, but does ministry in the secular environment where he works. He's a celebrity in my eyes because he is a man of integrity and prayer. He gets up early to pray. The way he lives his life is centered on being the very best steward of what God has given him. His joyful, positive attitude comes from his trust in the truth that God is for him. He inspires me to pursue a deeper relationship with the Lord. His success is eternal. I'm blessed to know him.

27 people like this

<u>**Comments:**</u>

None.

Day 25:
A True Celebrity

The Response

Celebrities in the media are idols. They have us sucked in so much that their lives matter more to us on a daily basis than regional, national, or global news. We care more about their gossip than about events that truly matter. Why do these people get to us? What exactly have they done for us besides entertained us?

Nothing against them, but I can think of a handful of REAL people in my life, in my circle of influence, who have impacted my life in far greater ways than the latest box office hit ever will. These are the people who get to us with their words and actions. They see us, hear us, pray for us, and no one wrote it out on a script, prompting them to do so. They don't get paid to care for us or give us their time. They make sacrifices that often go unnoticed.

nicky_farley: Hands down, my oldest son Matthew. He changed our lives forever in a matter of seconds! We went from an ordinary married couple to parents and never looked back. I will never ever, as long as I live, forget that moment when he was taken from my body and placed in my arms. He looked up at me and it was like nothing I'd ever felt. I love my little chicken!

_andrewlinton: A true celebrity in my opinion is my Cross Country and Long Distance Track Coach... Over the past four years in high school, he has been an incredible coach and has cheered me on every step of the way. He is one amazing coach. He treats our team like family and always knows the right thing to say that will put a smile on our faces. All I can say is, thanks for all the memorable memories through the many Cross Country and Track seasons we ran our hardest in.

mybubbles17: This guy is so amazing. [He] can make some amazing drinks at Starbucks and has a crazy love for Taylor Swift. But seriously, Cory is by far my favorite youth leader. He is always there to talk to and he brings you up when you are down. He is so encouraging. He is an amazing leader and worship leader. He is a great example of a follower of Christ. The list could go on and on. I am so blessed to have gotten closer to him and the rest of the youth group these past couple months. And Cory, please don't bop me on the head for using this picture!

Day 26:
An Activity to
De-Stress

leahmarieball:

Ok, this challenge is all about being real, so here it is: today I had a day from hell. Seriously. Seems ironic, right? There are many things I love to do when I'm stressed - music, laundry, running - but these are also all things I do when I'm *not* stressed. Here's the straight, raw truth: when I'm stressed, I watch *SpongeBob Squarepants* and drink chocolate milk. Candy is optional (for times when I'm super stressed). There you have it. Laugh if you want ... I'm going to go de-stress. This day seriously sucked and I feel crappy.

28 people like this

Comments:

☺   I feel you. When I'm stressed, I crave Pop Tarts©, Nutella© and Disney movies©. Sometimes all at once. Lol #butseriouslythough

☺   So I know we don't talk much but I've been following your photo challenge and I just want to say I think you're amazing. I love how open and honest you are and how willing you are to share your life.

☺   [Mine are] Chocolate Pop Tarts© and a romantic comedy.

☺   I think I'm going to do this. This past week hasn't been the best.

Day 26:
An Activity to
De-Stress

The Response

If it's only *distracting* you, it's not truly *de-stressing* you. I've learned this the hard way. There are things that we retreat to as a way to escape from all of life's bumps in the road, but we never get past those obstacles. We scoot around them or head back the other direction, or we stay where we are.

Exercise, boyfriends / girlfriends, food, movies, etc. - you name it. It's something that helps us release our tension, but doesn't help us get used to handling the traction. But worship has the power to not only calm and quiet us, but gives us the strength we need to take those bumps, dips, and walls head on. Full speed ahead, we're ready to go.

missmaddieroseee: I was going to put something else. Something light, goofy, or shallow, but everything aside from worship is distracting, not "de-stressing." There are so many ways we can worship. Art, dance, attitude, etc. My favorite way to worship is with my voice. I love playing piano, but there's something about singing His praises, and declaring His promises over my life that truly relieve my stress. I really just love to sing. That's where I started. I didn't know how to sing; I never knew what it meant to sing in key or how to hit a note. All I knew was how to shut my eyes and sing. Granted I am not the best, and there are probably a hundred people in the area alone that can sing better than me, but I love it. Last year I prayed God would give me the ability and desire to write my own songs. He gave me the gift of piano playing. After I got the hang of it, He gave me the gift to write. Through His gifts, I de-stress. And if others can benefit from it, glory to God.

invisiblecheers: Often when I'm stressed out or completely frazzled I have to pick up a sketch book or paintbrush to calm me down. It really helps me not to focus on really anything. When I make art, I'm in a zone you can't disturb and it really makes me a lot happier.

therealandrewyoung: Growing up, I would come home from school or work and go down to the basement to play drums for a few hours. It always helped me de-stress and take my mind off of things... I still do that to this day and I'm blessed to be able to do music for a living. God is good!

Day 27:
A Real Workout
Face

leahmarieball:

You know those workout pictures they use to "motivate" us with the perfectly toned chicks that don't have a drop of sweat on them? Or those posts entitled "working out" with an expression that reads pure bliss? I don't look or feel that way after a workout. Those pictures don't motivate me because I've learned that beauty isn't flawless, strength isn't painless, and real results require real work. Strong is beautiful, not skinny. Perseverance and hard work are motivational. The results are always worth it in the end. Like working out, anything we do in life should be done to our very best, and we should keep at it. My boot camp trainer puts it well: "Go hard or go harder; going home is not an option for you."

34 people like this

Comments:

☺   Just YES.

☺   Haha. My workout face is so ugly some lady in the gym the other day actually walked up to me and asked me if I was ok.

Day 27:
A Real Workout
Face

The Response

Motivational fitness accounts on Instagram reveal pictures of flawless, toned, shapely human beings with flat, rock-hard abs and perfectly sculpted muscles. Most of these people were just doused with a spray bottle of oil – "Now strike a pose and give me an expression that reads 'I just left the gym.'"

That's what we see and what we compare. But you can't forget that fitness and exercise are for our benefit, not for our bulk. If you're doing it right, and doing it in moderation, it takes time and patience. And if you're doing it right … you're not going to look glamorous.

Rad_rebekah: My first Color Me Rad 5k run. Talk about a work out.

karis_robinson: These are the three seniors on my basketball team…
Pretty much the only time I workout is when preparing for basketball or
playing basketball. Tonight was the last game of our season other than our
homecoming game. This makes me sad but I'm so proud of our team. We
worked our hardest and that's what matters.

iix.sydneylee: Wow, wow, wow. If this picture doesn't sum up my life,
I'm not sure what does. Since I'm not into the "normal" sports that usually

every other teen does, I get my workout in different ways. This picture was taken while we were baling hay, which if that's not a workout, I'm not sure what is. Everybody at least once in their life should throw around a couple hundred hay bales!

Day 28:
My Real Hair

leahmarieball:

It used to be filled with tight curls and the color of chestnut. Since the beginning of high school, however, it's been dyed every color minus blonde, cut every length, including a pixie cut, and worn in so many different styles, I should have written a book! Now it's just crazy/wavy like a lion's mane. Yeah, we'll go with that.

23 people like this

<u>**Comments:**</u>

☺   I tried the pixie. Never again. Lol. It's the only cut I've ever regretted. And I've tried them all too. I like it but then I miss being able to throw it into a ponytail when it's looking all crazy. I go back and forth between ponytail length and my current cut.

Day 28:
My Real Hair

The Response

Maybe I'm just jealous of all the women on social media who have these incredible hairstyles. There are even some guys online who sport better hairstyles than I do on my best day!

My hair is a curly, wavy, crazy mess - a lion's mane, a mermaid's nightmare. Even my brothers will spend a good chunk of time working gel and pomade through their hair, trying to get that "perfect" wave or swoop. It's no accident that sometimes the BEST thing you can do for your hair is leaving it alone. It needs to breathe. It needs to relax. It's ok to have "picture-imperfect" hair. Work it.

kleechristine: I'm the kind of person that cannot hide my true feelings well, which I'm ok with. My hair is a perfect example of that. It's always been a bit mane-like, and it surprises the hairdresser every time. I always hear exclamations of "Wow! There's a lot of this stuff!" It has been dyed every color from carrot top red to purple, even blonde during my middle-school punk-indie days. It is currently a honey/brownish-blondish-redish color. Just long enough to make me feel like I should drop out of school and become a professional mermaid. The thought has crossed my mind several times during finals week.

katelynn323: A crazy mess! Now… I'm going to straighten it!

Lizzyyybee: I can't really be bothered to do anything with it ever, so this is more just a normal #selfie… Two things I'm holding onto today: 1. There is a season and a time for everything. 2. Our bodies are temporary, but our souls are forever, and this crazy world is not my home.

Day 29:
An Insecurity

leahmarieball:

My insecurity is interaction / connection with other females. Whether it's my conversation, my humor, my likes / dislikes, I always feel inadequate. Even with the few girls that I'm close with right now, I feel inadequate as their friend. I do well in mixed groups but in groups with just women, I'm awkwardly silent. I don't know the reason why. I've been dealing with this since I was 13. Moving in my sister's shadow in high school has slightly transferred over into adulthood. I feel pitied and included only because of the family I come from and the influences around me. I'm thankful for who I have in my life, but this has been an ache in my heart for so long. I've learned I push it down and smother it. Whenever it comes up I isolate myself. The truth is, I feel judged by the very people who are concerned I'll judge them if they invite me out or include me. But I'm not perfect and I love people. I just want the opportunity to be myself. I want genuine friendships, not ones out of pity.

28 people like this

<u>**Comments:**</u>

☺   I sometimes feel the same way, but remember, "No one can make you feel inferior without your consent." You have so much light and love to offer that this alone will surely move those around you and make you impossible to ignore. Don't let anyone ever put out that light.

☺   I've always liked you for you! By the way, we're really overdue on our lunch!

☺   Every girl feels like her fellow female peers are judging her silently. I've always felt inferior to you in so many areas. I love you and I wouldn't change a thing about you.

☺   Ashley always talks about how much she admires you, your talents and your fashion. However, I feel just like that and have always struggled to make friends. I take everything personal and the way you hear women talk behind each other's backs furthers my fear that they are talking about me. That's why I've always loved being around you and Ashley. Your family was the only ones that could separate me from my family and truly see me for who I am as an individual. I always love hanging out with you! You know you are welcome anytime.

☺   Awh, I love you for YOU!

☺   I love you just so you know. You're wonderful.

☺   This further impresses on my heart the need for us to connect again soon. You are amazing.

☺ You're amazing. I admire how open you are to your flaws and insecurities. I need to be more like you girl. You're an inspiration!

☺ LOL WHAT! You are crazy. Miss you.

☺ Amen! I can really relate to that feeling ... It's so nice to hear that I'm not the only one. Thank you for opening up and sharing!

Day 29:
An Insecurity

The Response

Ah ... what to write in this small section of text. As I read through the posts that were included on Day 29, there was much insecurity that stood out, pricks of pain that people cringed to bring up. It was comforting to know that those reading were non-judgmental and offered encouragement. The best part about these posts was the overall consensus that staying down was not an option. They weren't going to let these things hold them back from living.

Read every caption listed below, but pay special attention to the last one: Juleah's testimony. She writes something powerful about insecurity. Her closing statements are the bottom line: "I AM A CHILD OF GOD." That's it. If everyone could know that, believe it, and apply it, insecurity wouldn't be a thing.

alexis_joy: Right now, an insecurity I have is people not viewing my worship as authentic. Anyone who has seen me worship knows that I like to jump and dance and I just get excited about the Lord's presence. I find joy in that. Though this is true, I am still human and I still have bad days. So for me, an insecurity is that people think I'm 'faking it' when I go up on stage and worship if I'm not feeling totally up to it. But I think I'm realizing that as long as I'm giving up everything that would hold me back, that's genuine worship. My God persists even in times where I'm sad or frustrated. Do I get judged for how I worship? Most likely, but I refuse to let that stop me from showing God how much I adore Him in the way that I do best. Through every season, God is still God and He is worthy of my praise.

racheljanethree: As much as I love to laugh and love being around people who make me laugh, my laugh is something I tend to be slightly insecure about. The Italian side of me tends to come out and it can sometimes be a little loud. On the flip side, I do love people who can laugh. There is something beautiful in seeing happiness spread across their face. No matter how silly I feel about myself, it will always be worth It if I can make someone else laugh.

jules_mirita: "What if people know?" One of my biggest insecurities WAS what if people knew my secret. What would they think? Would they look at me differently? Would they think I'm a bad person? Would they still think of me the same way? I was overwhelmed with insecurity and "what if's" of whether or not I would be accepted if people knew I had an eating disorder, so I hid it. The thing about insecurities are they are just lies. Their only purpose is to try and tell you that you are less than what you are TRULY worth. As I begin this journey of recovery I've learned that everything I thought, all of the insecurities, were lies laced with fear. Fear of never being good enough, or worth enough ... or perfect enough. I used to think that if people knew my "problem", or even that I was just recovering from this, they wouldn't love me. But that was just another lie. Tonight we did cardboard testimonies, and I faced my insecurity head on. In front of a chapel, I (along with other girls from my cabin) exposed the past. What was done tonight was amazing and I, along with many others, was freed tonight... So I used to be insecure about my past, and my current sickness, but I am unashamed to say that I am not perfect and that I am struggling. However this does not define me. I am a child of God, and I believe that He can heal me and get me out of this. I used to be insecure about my illness, and thought that if anyone knew I would be ruined, but I'm learning that I'm not alone in this struggle. So to anyone who sees this (and actually reads it) just know that you're not alone and you don't have to hide either.

Day 30:
My Smile

leahmarieball:

I have two smiles - both are genuine, but with one of them my nose crinkles up. I never noticed until it was lovingly pointed out to me. Have you ever noticed how powerful your smile is? Your smile has the potential to change the course of someone else's day. Women, and even some men, struggle with the concept of their smile, especially on social media. Instead we've resorted to mimicking ducks and the mascot of sour candy. Can we please change that? "I don't know what to do with my face when a picture is taken." I'll tell you what to do - throw out the "kissy" face and the "duck lips" and work what God gave you! Spread it around.

33 people like this

Comments:

☺   The crinkled nose smile is my favorite!

☺   So beautiful!

Day 30:
My Smile

The Response

You don't have to hide. You don't have to hide your smile either. Cameras trigger an automatic facial response from guys and girls alike. Guys give the smolder and girls pucker up. Why? I've done it too but why?

A smile is a powerful thing! Try it for a day. Flash it at the people that walk by you. It has the power to change someone's day, to light up that moment for him or her. Really … it does. It's so cool that the challenge starts with fresh-faces on Day 1 and ends with smiles on Day 30. Only God could do this.

The Result

Where do we go from here?

I can't speak for everyone, but I can tell you what "The [REAL] 30-Day Challenge" did for me.

As I write this today, I'm a completely different person than when I started the challenge.

No longer do I rely on make-up to hide my insecurities. I allow it to enhance my natural beauty, but that's as far as our relationship goes. I'm confident enough to let my real face show.

By the time this book is published, I will have shared the story of [REAL] six times in two different states: twice for two different youth groups, once for a high school, and three times for three different youth conferences. My unspoken dream is becoming reality. I believe it's only going to get bigger from here.

Relationships in my life are stronger and more vibrant. The person I secretly admire has been blessed beyond my words, and is now walking in faith, embarking upon the greatest adventure of her life. The relationship I have with my father, one that has never been very strong, has deepened since I posted that picture. He has been the most constant person in my lifetime and continues to be till this day. That handsome guy – the one pictured for the true celebrity post - well, let's just say he's planning out what the rest of his future is going to look like … and I get to do that with him! We were married in April 2015.

The events of my past - alcoholism, sexual sin, pornography, and depression - have been replaced with daily surrender of my will, an abundance of grace, love, intentional pursuit, and joy unspeakable. I no longer hide these things shamefully, but proudly display them as evidence of what my Savior can do. He reclaims broken items and restores them to the most extravagant works of art.

The struggles of my present - anxiety, fear, laziness, approval addiction, perfectionism, comparison, feelings of inadequacy, pride, lack of faith, and insecurity as a woman - are still things I'm working through, but I've recognized them to be real issues. I'm taking steps every day towards working out the positive and releasing the negative. It sounds so "self-help," but it's completely "Spirit-help." There's no way I would be able to move forward without the new-found confidence that I am fiercely loved, highly favored, deeply treasured, persistently adored and graciously chosen. That's what a relationship with God does for me and what [REAL] helped me realize.

Every morning I walk outside my front door, I realize how blessed I am, how much each day truly is a gift. There are new songs to sing, new people to meet, and new places to go.

Work is no longer a chore. That's definitely what it had become over the years, so much so that it was starting to eat away at my relationship with God and with others. As of December 2014, I stepped away from my position as a Worship Director, that "glorious" platform that I let go to my head and deem me unapproachable. Now I'm taking each day to learn who I really am in Christ, peeling back the remnants of the title, stuck to my identity. I'm learning what it means to worship and be a worship leader. I'm learning how to truly love and see people and hear them and walk with them through their pain, instead of nod and smile and walk away. Leading worship is an opportunity and a calling. Music is a second language that I get to use to speak into people's hurt and breathe healing. It's being used to break chains and set people free. With every strum of my guitar and note I sing, I'm seeing the embers of the flame glow brighter and brighter. And I'm doing it without a title.

People are no longer projects, tools, or problems in my eyes. They have the passion it takes to complete projects. They have the ability to be willingly used to accomplish great things. They have the potential to overcome incredible odds. But that's not their definition. Every person on this planet has a story. Every person on this planet markets that story differently, either with a loud voice or a whisper, with clean hands or multiple scars. But regardless of their delivery, personality, background or history, they … are … **valuable**.

"The [REAL] 30-Day Challenge" is about the individual. It's about me. It's about you. **It's about discovering whom the real you really is and unleashing that person. It's about setting that individual free!** It takes courage to do this. It takes turning off outside opinions, turning your back on the past, and running full-force into your destiny. But you can't discover what that looks like until you set your real self FREE. You won't discover who you really are until you are completely honest with yourself and transparent with others.

That's the **REAL ME**.

"The [REAL] 30-Day Challenge" is about people. Small groups, large groups, whole communities, an entire nation; it looks at the people within your circle of influence and it seeks to connect your stories with theirs. It celebrates the uniqueness, the gifts, the passions and desires, and the dreams of people all over the world. It takes real individuals and connects them together through real stories. It inspires authenticity and raises an army of world-changers. We can't do it alone and we weren't meant to do it alone. We need each other. It's about creating real relationships.

That's **REAL PEOPLE**.

"The [REAL] 30-Day Challenge" is about the world around you. From right outside your front door, down the street into your neighborhood, into your school or workplace, and as far as technology can take it. It has the potential to spread like a wildfire, clearing the way and making a noticeable difference. What *would* the world look like if people chose to remove the masks and stop playing pretend with each other? What would it look like if people chose to see bleeding hearts rather than walking shells?

That's **REAL LIFE**.

"The [REAL] 30-Day Challenge" is REAL ME, REAL PEOPLE, and REAL LIFE.

That's the vision.

The mission is simple: **to promote authenticity in the world of social media and provide an avenue for discovery and connection**.

How is this accomplished?

It starts with one. It moves into groups. It reaches the world.

Why authenticity?

Authenticity is the fire-starter to the inferno of identity. If we know our true identity, we fulfill our destiny.

Our identities have become so wrapped up in marketing what we *wish* we looked like, or accomplished, or did, or had, we've forgotten who we really are. **Some of us don't even know who that was to begin with.** Once the poison of inadequacy leaks into our veins, it doesn't take long for it to reach the core - our hearts. After that we have barely any energy left to look ourselves in the eyes when we see our reflection in the mirror.

We stop dreaming. We stop hoping. We stop caring.

"Are you saying that 'The [REAL] 30-Day Challenge' is the answer to all of that?"

Not at all.

This challenge can't revive dead dreams. It can't stop a heart from aching after it has been beaten down and trampled. It can't stop an addict from inserting one more needle or sucking down one more bottle. It won't keep eyes from wandering and lips from speaking lies.

But I believe in this because God gave it to me and I've seen His power through it, not just in my life, but also in the lives of people around me. It isn't just another photo challenge. It is not at all a way to "show off" or elevate your weaknesses and hurts so that people can feel sorry for you.

"The [REAL] 30-Day Challenge" is about answering the question: WHO ARE YOU?

Who do you think you are?

That isn't meant to come off as degrading; it's a real question.

What would your life look like if you could answer that question confidently? Wouldn't you like to know the answer?

The answer is the key to discovering your purpose here on the earth and fulfilling your destiny. It is the deepest cry of the heart because the heart was made for eternity. The heart was designed to long after - worship - the One for whom it was created.

Who is that person?

Well, He's not a person. He is Spirit. Not a wisp of air or flash of light or a good feeling. He's not in His creation or a mortal like us.

He is Divine. He is Holy. He is Just. He is Love. He is Truth. He is Savior. He is Father. He is Friend. He is Master, King, Lord, Ruler, Shepherd, Lover, Victor, Champion, Garden, Peace, Hope, Restorer, Redeemer, Deliverer, Healer, Creator, Maker, Sustainer, Provider … and more.

HE IS.

The only One who is good and perfect and holy - that is God.

God created you. He gave you life and breath and being and purpose.

God sustains you. He holds you and keeps you. He guards you and feeds you and clothes you.

God loves you.

You've heard it before. Most people have. But this isn't the line to a catchy song or a religious phrase that is tossed around to try and get people into a church building. It has been abused, misused, slandered, and taken out of context. But nothing that anyone has said or done can subtract from the depth of these words: **God loves YOU.**

He created you. Therefore He knows everything about you and He loves you as He designed you.

He sustains you. Therefore He knows what's coming for you, who you'll be, what you've done, and where you're going.

He loves you. Therefore He longs for you, pursues you, and won't give up until He has you.

That's why I believe in "The [REAL] 30-Day Challenge."

Even though it isn't a magical formula or a famous how-to that has amassed millions of success stories, **it has the mark of God on it and the love of Christ in it.** Please understand that I'm not saying that "The [REAL] 30-Day Challenge" is the perfect answer, or the answer at all! I am not claiming it is faultless or blameless or that it will solve every problem known to mankind. That is *not* the message. God uses people all over this world to make a difference, to raise awareness, to help people, to show them His love. That's all that this is.

"The [REAL] 30-Day Challenge" is ONE more way that He is pursuing you, chasing you, and longing for your heart.

Let's face it: this world is slowly killing itself. Our generation and the one to come are in trouble. We're overdosing on technology and all it offers us. We drink it in and everything that comes with it. We're not satisfied until we've let everyone everywhere know our "business," posted a picture that tells the story, and in 140 characters depicted a circumstance in the most vague manner possible. Why?

So that people pursue us.

Can't you see it? Don't you realize that you do it, that I do it, that we are all doing it? We're all craving affirmation, approval, and recognition because it shows that people are watching and "liking" and giving us their time. It reveals a slight degree of pursuit, and in this day and age we'll take whatever we can get! It doesn't matter if we have to dress ourselves up, purchase the latest gadgets, go to the most exotic places, and constantly have our cell phones with us to document it. As long as we prove to everyone tuning in that we're exciting, we're intelligent, we're beautiful or handsome, we're good people, we're doing something worthwhile, and that … **We're worth it**.

We just want to be worth it. We want to have value. But more than that, we want to know we have value.

But the truth is … **YOU ALREADY DO**.

Your identity isn't found in what you think you look like or what other people think of your appearance. Your identity isn't found in stuff. Your identity isn't found in how many friends you have or how many "likes" your pictures get over social media. Your identity isn't the places you've been, the accomplishments you can brag over, the degree you received from that one university, or the career you always wanted. It doesn't increase based on what you acquire, it doesn't decrease based on what you lose. It doesn't diminish with your health, it doesn't expand with your influence, it doesn't depend upon your wealth or lack thereof.

The world will tell you that it does, but this is a **LIE.**

Technology isn't evil, but it can be misconstrued. The trend in technology is a counterfeit of appearance, material possessions, accomplishments, and wealth. On one hand it gives us bragging rights, but on the other it leaves a hole inside that we strive to fill. It creates a false sense of identity. Because of this the human race is starving and the best solution at our fingertips results in a zombie nation glued to their phones.

I think God has had enough.

Not with us. God has had enough of the lies we believe and how easily we suck them into our core. I believe He has had enough of the media telling us how to live our lives and what success looks like and what value we have in their eyes. I believe He has had enough of thousands of teens and young adults committing suicide, overdosing, feeling rejected, giving up, and letting go of their dreams. He has had enough of His kids giving in to a world that celebrates sexual sin, rebellion, drunkenness, lust, pride, selfishness, greed, self-righteousness, love of money, and love of pleasure. He has had enough of the identity crisis that's slowly taking over His beloved creation, His coveted prize.

How can He reach us? **I believe He has to get inside our technology.**

He's not old-fashioned or out-of-date. He knows all things and understands all things, more so than anything we will or could ever know or understand. He knows what we're into now and what's coming in the future. Technology is child's-play for Him.

There are so many applications that God is inspiring in so many people all over the world that are and will be downloaded into our iPhones or Androids, onto our MacBook's or laptops, and easily accessible through any means of technology. He's using men and women alike to fashion His ideas and His means of contact to reach a very technologically savvy generation. They do this through different methods, but they ultimately communicate the same message:

GOD LOVES YOU.

If God loves you, He loves all of you. If He loves all of you, He's ready and willing to do whatever it takes to get to you, to reach you, and to pursue you.

When God sent His Son, Jesus Christ, to this earth - to take on the punishment for our sins, to die on a cross, and be raised again to life so that we might have the opportunity to be in relationship with Him - He was portraying the immense love God the Father has for all mankind. God didn't give us a carbon copy of Himself, a replica, or a counterfeit - He gave us **HIMSELF, ALL OF HIMSELF**, so that we would know that **HE LOVES US**.

God is ready and willing to go to great lengths to pursue your heart, to show you that He hasn't given up on you and that He holds your identity.

What is your identity?

You can't answer that question on your own. I can't answer it. "The [REAL] 30-Day Challenge" can't answer it. Only God can answer that question and He already has. When He gave Himself, all of Himself for you, He was offering you a choice - the world or His Son, death or life. God holds the answer, and when we turn to God to help us answer that question, He does so.

"You are my son."

"You are my daughter."

This is who you are.

You are not your greatest fears or your darkest failures. You were bought, purchased with the highest price, the life of His perfect Son. He went to the greatest lengths for you. He literally died for you. And nothing can take that away from you.

You are who He says you are.

"The [REAL] 30-Day Challenge" was given to me first as a personal challenge - "Leah, who do you think you are?" It was a reevaluation of my heart.

Every Sunday I stood on a platform before hundreds of people. Every Sunday I would sing familiar worship tunes, looking fantastic in skinny jeans and mile-high heels, and don a pretty smile that would never flip, even if someone paid me a snarky remark. But who I really was remained a mystery. I rarely reached anyone. I rarely helped anyone. My friendliness was nice, but it never made a lasting impact. It wasn't until I found myself in a parking lot, listening to the shaky voice of a dear friend uncover her wounds, that I discovered how counterfeit really was my life.

Who can relate to someone who has it altogether? Who can relate to someone who is seemingly perfect?

God wasn't going to fix what I claimed wasn't broken. When I was dishonest before others, whether in reality or through social media, I misrepresented my true identity and all He had done to reclaim that for me. Why would I do that? I believed lies over the Truth. I chose to wallow in self-pity and hide behind the walls of pride. Then one day God had enough. He used a broken individual to chisel away at my calloused heart.

He used her story to get to me and show me that "perfection" in humans is unapproachable.

But brokenness …

Brokenness - admitting that we're wrong, that we don't have it altogether, and that we need help - is inviting.

It invites strong people to sit with us and share in our pain and lift us up when we're too weak to stand. It invites other broken people to realize that they're not alone and that they too can get the help they need. It invites the Lord to come in and heal us and restore us to the glory for which we were destined!

Authenticity requires recognizing and revealing brokenness because we are broken people.

I'm not saying that authenticity is mainly openness about your dirty past so that you can gain sympathy and misguided attention. It's not putting your "junk" out there and having a social pity party. Authenticity is being who you truly are, and in that, you realize that brokenness is apart of being human. And in your brokenness, you are able to accept and give out grace.

"The [REAL] 30-Day Challenge" is about bringing authenticity back into the world of social media, where the very topic has become a foreign language. But when wielded with confidence, authenticity has the power to transform individuals, to connect groups of people, and to inspire change in the world around us.

When God gave me "The [REAL] 30-Day Challenge," it was initially for me to rediscover my identity in Him by revealing parts of myself that I had kept hidden for so long. It wasn't the end of all my imperfection, but the beginning of my healing from feeling the need to be perfect. It was the beginning of loving myself, and in turn, loving other flawed people.

After God gave me "The [REAL] 30-Day Challenge," I realized it wasn't just for me; it was for everyone. It's just one more way that God wants to show this technological generation that He hasn't given up on them. It's one more way that God is pursuing us and getting down onto our level so that we discover our destinies.

It's one more way that God is saying: **"I love you. The REAL you."**

Conclusion:
Take the Challenge

You've read my story. You've read the stories of others.

Now it's your turn.

Whether you picked this up in a bookstore somewhere or purposely purchased it, whether you're completely convinced or aren't sold at all, I'm challenging you.

I dare you to take the challenge and watch what will happen.

Since its creation, "The [REAL] 30-Day Challenge" has expanded. What used to be one for all has now multiplied into two, one for guys and one for girls. They're gender-specific because I've realized that both audiences have different desires and needs.

Also since its creation, our team and myself have realized the need to eliminate one of the major rules of the challenge: black and white photos only. Because there is a black and white filter on Instagram and on most photo editing applications, this rule really confused people more than it helped them catch the overall vision of [REAL]. Therefore, since color photos are not the issue (filters are the issue), we decided to expand to color photos.

This is only the beginning.

You've gotten this far into the book for a reason. You're meant to take this challenge, no matter who you think you are or what you think you know about yourself. Maybe you're confident in your identity. Take the challenge and watch that confidence soar. Maybe you feel so far removed from who you are that you doubt anything could change whatsoever. Take the challenge and get ready for God to do something because He will. But He won't invade your space and He won't force you to do anything against your will.

This part is left in your hands.

In the remaining pages, you'll find all the information you need to get connected with "The [REAL] 30-Day Challenge," as well as the challenge lists for guys and girls.

This is it - your moment, your move.

Keep it [REAL].

Resources

Take the challenge! Invite a friend to take it with you. Post your photos to social media using the hashtag #real30daychallenge.

www.real30day.com

Day 1 - Let's Be [REAL]
Day 2 - A Walk in My Shoes
Day 3 - When I grow up
Day 4 - Secret Jam
Day 5 - Chick Flick
Day 6 - De-Stressing Activity
Day 7 - Portrait of a [REAL] Person
Day 8 - My View When I'm Working
Day 9 - A Bad Habit
Day 10 - The [REAL] Me Wishes I Could Be
Day 11 - A True Celebrity
Day 12 - My Love Language
Day 13 - A Regret
Day 14 - A Family Member(s) I Admire
Day 15 - A Transformation

Day 16 - Something I Grieve Over
Day 17 - What Inspires Me
Day 18 - Fast & Furious
Day 19 - What Really Happened
Day 20 - Pick-up Lines
Day 21 - Unspoken Dream
Day 22 - An Addiction [PAST]
Day 23 - Favorite Scripture, Quote, or Lyric
Day 24 - An Addiction [PRESENT]
Day 25 - An Unbelievable Moment
Day 26 - Great Dads
Day 27 - She's Perfect
Day 28 - A Mirror Pic
Day 29 - "Lip Service"
Day 30 - [REAL] Challenge Transformation

NO FILTERS

NO MANIPULATION

NO COVER-UPS

www.real30day.com

Day 1 - Fresh-Face Selfie
Day 2 - An Unspoken Dream
Day 3 - Someone I Secretly Admire
Day 4 - What Really Happened
Day 5 - Outside My Front Door
Day 6 - Secret Jam
Day 7 - Portrait of a [REAL] Person
Day 8 - My View When I'm Working
Day 9 - A Bad Habit
Day 10 - A Weakness
Day 11 - "Lip Service"
Day 12 - My Love Language
Day 13 - An Addiction [PAST]
Day 14 - An Addiction [PRESENT]
Day 15 - A Regret

Day 16 - A Family Member I Admire
Day 17 - A Transformation
Day 18 - Something I Grieve Over
Day 19 - A Walk in My Shoes
Day 20 - What Inspires Me
Day 21 - First Thought in the Morning
Day 22 - Favorite Scripture, Quote, or Lyric
Day 23 - OOTD [Outfit of the Day]
Day 24 - A 'Mirror" Pic
Day 25 - A True Celebrity
Day 26 - An Activity to De-stress
Day 27 - A [REAL] Workout Face
Day 28 - My [REAL] Hair
Day 29 - An Insecurity
Day 30 - My Smile

NO FILTERS

NO MANIPULATION

NO COVER-UPS

Visit our website at…

real30day.com

Check out [REAL] on these other social media platforms:

FACEBOOK:

facebook.com/
real30daychallenge

TWITTER:

twitter.com/real30day

INSTAGRAM:

instagram.com/real30day

Want to share your story? Feel free to get in touch with us at…

E-MAIL:

mail@real30day.com

Printed in the United States
By Bookmasters